Foal Breeding
for Beginners

Foal Breeding
for Beginners

A **Step-by-Step** Guide
for the First-Time
Horse Breeder

LAINEY CULLEN-MCCONKEY

author of *The Ultimate Guide to Horse Health & Care*

Skyhorse Publishing

All photos copyright © Lainey Cullen-McConkey unless otherwise noted
    Page ix, 25, 49, 71, 100, 101, 102, 130, 131, 136, Jack McConkey
    Page 8, Heather Pope, Kaotic Kreations

Skyhorse Publishing books may be purchased in bulk at special discounts for sales promotion, corporate gifts, fund-raising, or educational purposes. Special editions can also be created to specifications. For details, contact the Special Sales Department, Skyhorse Publishing, 307 West 36th Street, 11th Floor, New York, NY 10018 or info@skyhorsepublishing.com.

Skyhorse® and Skyhorse Publishing® are registered trademarks of Skyhorse Publishing, Inc.®, a Delaware corporation.

Visit our website at www.skyhorsepublishing.com.

10 9 8 7 6 5 4 3 2 1

Library of Congress Cataloging-in-Publication Data is available on file.

Cover design by Daniel Brount
Cover photo by gettyimages

Print ISBN: 978-1-5107-5088-3
Ebook ISBN: 978-1-5107-5089-0

Printed in China

To steal from a song:
"This is dedicated to the one I love"

This is for my husband Jack, the amazing man who has been the rock and support that enabled me to write this book, along with my first book.

But more than that, he is my collaborator, my backup, my cheerleader, and my willing partner when we started the journey of breeding our first foal. Without his encouragement I don't think either the foal or the books would have ever happened.

Thank you, my love, for putting up with it all!

Lainey
X

Contents

About the Author

MY name is Lainey Cullen-McConkey, and I have been riding/working with horses since I was a teenager, so now more than thirty years. Over the years I have ridden many different types of horses and ponies, in many different styles (dressage, jumping, cross-country, side saddle, Western) and was also involved for a number of years as a member of the British team which entered a rather unique horse race in France called La Route du Poisson (Google it!).

I currently own, or rather am owned by, a palomino Quarter Horse mare named Color WithinTheLines (Barbie), an off-track Thoroughbred mare named Moyie, and Moyie's newest son, Moyie's Royal Outlaw (Geo), who is half Thoroughbred, half APHA. Plus, of course two dogs, ~~four~~ five cats (and I'm no longer allowed to go to the animal shelter unsupervised), chickens, parakeets, fish, turtles, etc.

All of these critters live with my husband Jack and me on our ranch, and between us we manage to make it all work!

Introduction

LET me just say right up front that this is *not* any kind of textbook on breeding horses, but is intended more as a guide for what to expect from your first foray into breeding. If you are looking for a good factual veterinary type book, I highly recommend Peter Rossdale's *The Horse from Conception to Maturity*. This was my go-to book from before my mare was even pregnant.

With this book I will give you an insight into breeding your first foal, regardless of how experienced you are in other aspects of horse management. I've been riding/training/working with horses for more than thirty years, but this was my first time breeding a foal of my own, and it really made me realize just how little I knew on the subject. While this book broadly covers the foal's life from even before conception to backing, I'm not going to get super deep into the starting and backing part, partly because there are a whole lot of other resources available for that, but mostly because that subject covered in detail would be a whole book in itself. But we'll touch on the important points, at least as I see them.

You will get to know your mare *way* more intimately than you ever expected to through this process, so if you're put off by icky things, breeding your own may not be for you! But I guess if you make it through some of the terms used in this book (and even more so if you also pick up a textbook on foaling) then you're partway there, so let's move on to the foal breeding journey we started back in 2015.

Chapter 1

Decisions, Decisions

Why Are You Breeding?

When you first decide to breed your mare, the first and most important question you have to ask yourself is *why* you want to breed a foal. I know, it seems pretty obvious. You're breeding because you want a "free" horse. Let me set you straight on that one. Breeding a foal is *not* going to get you a free horse. Probably not even a cheap one! Factor in the stud fee for use of the stallion, the extra feeding which your mare will require during pregnancy and even more so afterward when she's feeding a hungry baby, the extra vaccinations required (though this is a little dependent on where you are in the world), extra vet visits, and the potential emergency vet visits at foaling time and extra farrier care, all in all, breeding a foal is *not* something to be undertaken on a tight budget.

If you're not looking for a free/cheap horse, you may want to breed your mare because she's awesome and you want another one. Now, this one is a little trickier for me because in a way that is why I bred Moyie. But I'll get back to that. Just bear in mind that genetics are tricky and just because your beloved mare is a wonderful jumping/dressage/show horse doesn't necessarily mean that baby will follow suit. There are plenty of anecdotes about fabulous racing mares being bred to fabulous racing stallions and producing offspring that couldn't outrun a tortoise. Okay, that's an exaggeration, but you get my point. (Also, we have a few wild gopher tortoises who live on our ranch, and they can actually move pretty fast when they have a mind to.)

You may choose to breed your mare because she is no longer able to work/compete for some reason, perhaps a permanent injury. Obviously in this instance you must coordinate with your vet to make certain that your mare is still capable of safely carrying a foal to term. It is always possible that a severe leg injury would make the added weight of a foal and all the associated placenta/fluids just too much for her to bear.

One other reason many people choose to breed their mare, quite an old-fashioned reason, is to "improve" the mare's temperament. I'm not sure how much science there is to support this, but it was certainly often done in the old days to try to "cure" a very hormonal, cranky mare. Of course, then you run the risk that a very antisocial mare will, instead of becoming a sweet and nurturing mother, reject or even attack her own foal (I know of at least one mare who deliberately trampled her foal to death). So, if one of your objectives is to make a mean mare nicer, just be very aware that you may instead find yourself with a mean mare *and* a foal which needs to be bottle-fed and hand-raised!

Moyie came to me in extremely poor condition, and it took almost six months to get her back into any kind of reasonable shape. Since I first met this pathetic little soul, Moyie blossomed into an outstanding mare with the most amazing temperament. I should also mention that Moyie was born in 1994, so when she foaled in May 2016, she was twenty-two years old. I know this sounds quite old to put her through the rigors of pregnancy and foaling, but the idea of breeding her had been approved by our vet before we even

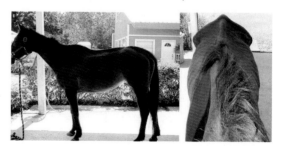

May 21, 2012

January 9, 2017

started on our journey. Moyie was twenty-one years old when we put her in foal, but she has had at least two foals in the past, which makes the process a little easier on her than if she'd been a maiden mare.

Check Out Those ~~Jeans~~ Genes

For whatever reason you've decided to breed your mare, before you get too starry-eyed at the prospect of a foal, take a good, long, objective look at your mare. Think about it very carefully and try to be brutally honest. Is her conformation good enough to pass on to another generation? I know it's hard, because we tend to see only the good in our "babies" but try to look at her like a stranger (or, if you truly can't be objective, ask your trainer or vet or another less emotionally involved person). Are her legs good? Is she cow hocked or otherwise not "textbook?" (Although this does actually vary a bit by breed/type. For example, good hindleg confirmation in a Clydesdale would be considered cow hocked in other breeds!) How about her forelegs? Good shoulder? You get the idea. Also, don't go thinking, "She has a really short back, so I'll put her to a stallion with a really long back—that should get me a foal with an average back!" There are some much more important considerations when it comes to genetics, and those pertain to inheritable diseases. I don't want to delve *too* deeply into this subject, but there are definitely some things you should know. There are some breed-specific genetic disorders, and fortunately the horse may be tested for many of these to see whether they carry the specific genes which cause the condition.

A horse may be:

- *Heterozygous,* carrying one copy of the relevant gene;
- *Homozygous positive,* carrying two copies of the gene; or
- *Homozygous negative,* not carrying the defective gene at all

Additionally, it must be understood that genes also vary, being classified as either recessive, dominant, or incomplete dominant. A *recessive* gene means that the horse must be homozygous positive, having two copies of the defective gene, to suffer from the disease. This means that both mare and stallion must carry at least one copy of the mutated gene for the foal to be affected. A foal born with one defective copy and one non-defective copy of the gene is a carrier, with a 50 percent chance of any future offspring also having the defective gene. A *dominant* gene is one which may be passed on and affect the foal even if only one parent has the defective gene. *Incomplete dominant* means that a homozygous positive (two copies) horse *will* pass the gene to all of their progeny, regardless of the other parent's status. A heterozygous horse has a 50 percent chance of passing along the defective gene, and a homozygous negative horse does not carry the defective gene and therefore *cannot* pass it along (but if the other parent is homozygous positive, the foal *will* inherit the defective gene from this parent).

Very often these days a breeder will have each foal tested at a fairly young age, and in fact the AQHA mandated that any foal who was born after January 1, 1998 and who is descended from the stallion Impressive *must* be tested for HYPP[1] and their results are then shown on their registration certificate. Results are shown as N/N (negative) meaning that the horse is normal and will never be affected by HYPP or pass it on to progeny, or N/H (heterozygous positive) which means that if the horse is bred to a N/N horse, there is a 50 percent chance of producing an affected foal. The final test result is H/H (homozygous positive) which means that the horse is severely affected and any future foals *will* be affected, regardless of the other parent. AQHA rules do not permit the registration of H/H foals born since 2007, so if your mare is a Quarter Horse born after January 1, 1998, then her registration papers will show her HYPP status. If she is older than this then she may not have been tested.

The genetic disorders below should be tested for. Testing is pretty straightforward. You send a hair sample (usually thirty to forty mane hairs complete with root follicles) to a laboratory that does this work. The one I have found most useful is Animal Genetics (animalgenetics. us). They offer a wide range of tests, including tests for color genes as well as genetic disorders. I would certainly say that the disorders are much more important to know about than color, but many stallion owners list the details of their stallion's color genes, since some genes indicate that a foal will inherit a particular characteristic of that stallion, so let me touch on it quickly.

As an example, Most Wanted Outlaw, the stallion we used, is homozygous for both the Tobiano gene (TT) and the black allele (EE), meaning that he will always produce Tobiano foals, and these foals will always have black as their base color. (Regardless of "actual" color, all horses have either black or red as their base color.) Outlaw is also heterozygous for the agouti gene (Aa) which, simply put, pushes the black to the "points" of the horse, so the information that

---

1 Hyperkalemic Periodic Paralysis.

Outlaw's owner provides lists that he is FIVE PANEL NN, LWO NN, EE, TT, Aa. This information helps a mare owner with their stallion selection if they are hoping to breed a specific color of foal.

Now, the FIVE PANEL is related to the genetic disorder side of things, so we'll look at that now. The genetic disorders most commonly tested for in Quarter Horses and related breeds are often grouped into what is known as The FIVE PANEL:

- Glycogen Branching Enzyme Deficiency (GBED)
- Hereditary Equine Regional Dermal Asthenia (HERDA)
- Hyperkalemic Periodic Paralysis disease (HYPP)
- Malignant Hyperthermia (MH)
- Polysaccharide Storage Myopathy—Type 1 (PSSM1)

In Paint horses (which are often related to the Quarter Horse) additional testing may be carried out for genetic disorders including Lethal White Overo (LWO).

Arabians and related breeds are tested for a three panel (though it actually covers four disorders):

- Cerebellar Abiotrophy (CA)
- Lavender Foal Syndrome (LFS)
- Severe Combined Immunodeficiency (SCID)
- Foal Immunodeficiency Syndrome (FIS)

I'm not going to delve into the details of all of these disorders. Suffice it to say that if it has been deemed necessary to develop a genetic test for something, it's not something you want to deliberately breed!

To sum all of this up a bit more succinctly:

- If your mare falls under a breed which should be tested for genetic abnormalities, the time to find out if she is affected or a carrier is *before* breeding her.

- Make sure your chosen stallion is also free from these defective genes. If he hasn't been tested, I would recommend avoiding him, just to be safe.

Choosing a Stallion

Once we'd decided to put Moyie in foal, then of course we had to select a stallion. Choosing a stallion really depends on what you're looking for from the breeding. Always bearing in mind the caveats above, I have to say that the first thing which should be considered is location. Some stallion owners do offer artificial insemination with chilled/frozen semen, or obviously you can go the old-fashioned way and do live cover. If you're going the AI route, location isn't so important as the semen will be shipped to you, but you do need to have a vet who is experienced in carrying out insemination services. If you want to do live cover, obviously picking a stallion in Texas if you live in Vancouver isn't going to be ideal.

I knew that I would have to send my mare away to be bred and that she would have to stay away for a week or so, but I wanted her as close as possible, which meant keeping my search limited to my home in Florida. I have always loved paint horses, so my first choice was to find a paint stallion. The Internet is a wonderful thing, and by searching on some sites I was able to find a couple of potential stallions. The other thing I wanted was to keep some height in the foal, since I do like bigger horses. Moyie is around 16.1hh, and I wanted a stallion at least that tall, but as it turned out, the one we chose was only 15hh.

The other very important aspect of the stallion you should take into consideration is their temperament. Bear in mind the old adage "handsome is as handsome does." Some stallions have less-than-friendly temperaments, which is why you need to try to visit them before making a decision so that you can gauge their behavior. I know, you may think that so long as he doesn't hurt your mare then it's fine, but if the stallion is aggressive or mean-spirited, there's always the chance of the foal being the same way, though I know at least one lovely stallion whose oldest son was pretty mean, so it can throw back to a previous generation. If your mare's sire was mean, it may pass down to her foal even though the stallion you use is sweet. I do not adhere to the belief that a bad attitude is acceptable if the horse is good at their job. If a stallion is aggressive, I don't care what his bloodlines are, he needs to be a gelding!

As an example of the type of temperament I would consider "good," one of the horses I take care of is an Arabian stallion. This horse is happiest when he is out in his field 24–7, but this past winter we had a rare and severe thunderstorm (not that thunderstorms are all that rare in Florida, but in winter they're pretty unusual). The storm wasn't forecast to be as severe as it became, so I had left the stallion out until the storm woke me around two in the morning. Now, when you have a mature stallion who you can lead from field to barn with his lead rope in one hand and a flashlight in the other in the middle of a nighttime thunderstorm, that's the kind of behavior that earns them the right to remain a stallion!

So, with location, color, height, and temperament front and center in mind, the stallion we chose was Most Wanted Outlaw. He was only four years old when we bred Moyie with him, but he had already sired

Most Wanted Outlaw

some gorgeous foals so his stallion abilities were well proven. Now, I broke one of my own rules by not meeting the stallion in person before making my final choice. We got lucky, finding Outlaw to be not only well put together but also very good-minded with a wonderfully calm temperament. But, as I said before, make the effort to go meet the horse if at all possible, and if you're not allowed to get close to him, even when his handler is with him, remove him from your list. If those who deal with him daily don't trust him, why should you?

I think that pretty much covers the issue of choosing your mare's new boyfriend (or at least her one-night stand). To me, the most important criterion is temperament, then conformation, location, and care. Color, while I was certainly aiming for a paint foal, is truly very far down the list. You probably know the old saying "a good horse is never a bad color," and it's very true. Yes, you can try to get a specific color (and there are some nice free online color probability websites) but if you're really going to be upset at getting a nice healthy chestnut foal when you were trying for a palomino, then you have no business breeding a foal. Even if our foal had been born solid colored, I would not have taken the Outlaw's owner Amber up on her colored foal guarantee. All I wanted was a healthy foal and mare at the end of the process.

Another consideration you must make when deciding to send your mare to stud is to be certain that she will be well cared for while she is there. If the other horses at the premises seem healthy and happy (and don't discount the value of happiness) then the chances are pretty good that your mare will also be well taken care of. This should be particularly obvious if, as in my situation, the stallion owner has a number of different mares coming and going. Yes, when mares are in heat and the stallion knows exactly why they're there, you have to expect some yelling and excitable behavior (from both sides of the gender gap!) but it should be easy to see if the horses are in good shape. For my own part (and even as a very nervous and paranoid horse mommy) I had no hesitation in leaving my mare in Amber's very capable and kind hands.

As a little anecdote of the kind of thing I mean, while Moyie was there (her second visit, which we'll get to in a minute) she managed to get a large wooden splinter in her chest. Not a big deal, happens very easily, but by chance Amber noticed it while taking Moyie to the vet to be checked to see if she was ovulating. She had her vet surgically remove the splinter and simply sent me a photo of the offending article. No fuss, and no bill for the minor procedure. Just chalked up to "one of those things." You want someone who will look after your mare in the way you do, and that's precisely what we found.

Let me add just one more thought to this. Be as objective as you possibly can in the stallion selection process. Don't allow yourself to "make allowances" for a stallion with a poor temperament or perhaps some kind of conformation problem (though hopefully a horse with poor conformation isn't being used as a stallion!) just because you *want* to use him. Do you really want to take the chance on the resultant foal either having a physical problem or just being, let's be honest, a bit of a brat (okay, I took out the word I really wanted to use!) just because of a stallion's bloodlines? I know I wouldn't. I've heard people with high quality performance horses say that their horse is horrible to handle on the ground, with awful manners, but say it's okay "because he performs great in the ring." You will spend far more time handling your horse than competing with them. I would rather have a well-mannered horse who couldn't jump a twig than a Grand Prix showjumper I couldn't trust.

Now that we have a bit of a background in place about the whole process, let's move on to the main event. Or rather, a couple of main events followed by many months of nail-biting before the *main* main event!

Chapter 2

The Journey Begins

Breeding Contracts

After deciding on the stallion, I contacted his owner to discuss the breeding, and after some discussions we had a signed contract in place. It it is very important that you have a signed breeding contract in place so that both you and the stallion owner know exactly what is expected from each other. The contract should at least offer a NFFR (No Foal Free Return) guarantee, meaning that if your mare does not produce a foal after having been checked and confirmed to be *in* foal, then you can rebreed to the stallion at no additional stud fee (though you may still have to pay additional "keep" charges). Some stallion owners may still offer a NFNF (No Foal No Fee) guarantee, which is as straightforward as it sounds, but I think these days most offer NFFR.

Outlaw's owner goes a couple of steps further with her contract, offering LCFG, which is a Live Colored Foal Guarantee. This is not only guaranteeing that your mare will produce a live foal (under these guarantees the definition of a live foal is usually one which gets to its feet and nurses from the mare) but also that the foal will fall under the definition of "colored" under APHA rules, which generally means that the foal will have white *somewhere* on the body or upper legs or mane/tail which qualifies it as a paint horse. White markings on the lower legs or face aren't necessarily going to qualify a horse as being colored. Although genetics are tricky, as I said, horses can be genetically tested to verify if they carry a specific color gene, and Outlaw is homozygous for both black and tobiano, meaning that he is guaranteed to produce paint foals. A horse can *genetically* be a Paint horse but appear to be a solid color. (A horse I once thought was a thoroughbred by his appearance was actually a "solid" Paint!)

The breeding contract may also include a clause which requires you to provide proof that your mare has been checked for sexually transmittable diseases, which is done by taking swabs from her cervix and clitoral fossa/sinuses. (This is also routinely done on stallions, where the urethra, urethral fossa, and sheath are swabbed.) The diseases checked for include:

- CEM—contagious equine metritis
- EVA—equine viral arteritis
- Klebsiella pneumoniae
- Pseudomonas aeruginosa

Horses may be infected with these diseases by sexual contact with an infected horse or, in the case of CEM, a foal may actually be born as a carrier of the disease, so even at his first use as a stallion a colt foal born as a carrier would be capable of passing on the disease. For this reason, both mare and stallion should be swabbed at least once each year. In the case of EVA, the fluids which are present at birth may also present a source of infection, so the area must be thoroughly cleaned/disinfected before other mares are allowed to enter the area.

As with any other legally binding contract, make sure that you thoroughly read the contract before signing, and if you are unclear on anything, *ask*!

Live Cover or AI?

Mares can be bred in a couple of different ways. The first and most obvious breeding method is live cover. So, what is "live cover"? Just like it sounds, your mare is covered, bred, by a stallion in the natural way. Let's face it, horses have been breeding for millennia without human help, so I think they have a pretty good handle on the whole thing. Of course, most places aren't going to just throw the mares in a field with a stallion and let them have at it, partly because that can make it difficult to know exactly when a particular mare has been covered, and also (mainly) as this opens both stallion and mare up to possible injuries. Trust me, when a mare *isn't* in the mood, she will make no bones about it, and stallions have been seriously injured or even killed by mares in this way.

"Teasing" or the seduction process

Live cover is more often done in a more controlled way, with both mare and stallion being controlled by handlers. Now, breeders have different approaches to this, but I'll briefly outline what I would consider to be the "traditional" way of doing things. The mare needs to be "teased" to check whether she is receptive to the stallion. This generally involves leading the two horses to opposite sides of a sturdy wall, where the stallion is allowed to interact with the mare in a safe environment. He will usually start at her neck and shoulder area, sniffing and licking his way along to her hindquarters, maybe nipping her gently with his teeth. Both horse handlers need to be alert to how the horses are behaving, keeping an eye on how the mare is reacting to the stallion's attentions. Fortunately, most mares are less than subtle about these things. If she *isn't* in estrus (or in heat, in season, or any other term that may be used in your region of the world) then the mare may react quite violently, squealing and kicking out in the stallion's direction (hence the need for the sturdy wall between them!). If she *is* in estrus, she will react quite differently, spreading her hind legs, raising her tail, and generally showing that she is receptive to the stallion's advances. Mares will often also pass a thick yellow urine at this stage. This urine is rich in pheromones which confirm to the stallion that she is indeed ready

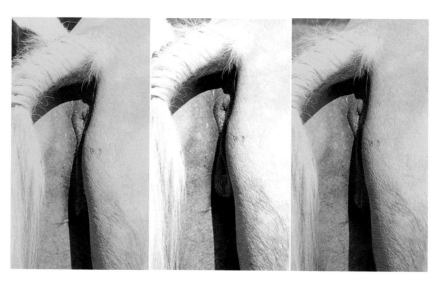

"Winking"

to mate. She will also display "winking" behavior, which means that she everts the lips of her vulva to expose the clitoris (you will sometimes see mares do this after urinating, but that doesn't necessarily mean she is in season all the time).

Some breeders keep a stallion, often a pony, for the sole purpose of teasing mares (though they will generally allow him to breed the occasional mare just to keep him interested in his job). Using a horse specifically as a teaser means that the breeder need not risk injury to a high value stallion at the teasing wall but can just bring him into play when the mare is confirmed to be receptive. I always feel sorry for teaser stallions, though, because they are like the perpetual wingman, always getting the girl for someone else!

If the mare isn't in season, she will be tried again on subsequent occasions until she *is* receptive to the stallion. If things don't seem to be progressing on a normal schedule, veterinary intervention may then be required (this is what I had to do, so I will touch on that in a bit), but if the mare is in season, yippee! At this stage many breeders will quickly wrap the mare's tail to keep it out of the way (believe it or not, a stallion can sustain a painful wound to his penis if one of the mare's tail hairs gets in the way). Some mares will also have covering boots placed on their hind feet. These are thick felt booties which provide some padding if the mare *does* kick at the stallion (sort of like boxing gloves for horses).

At this point breeders vary on just how much assistance they offer. Some breeders will just have the mare held and lead the stallion up to let him do his job. This is usually quite easy with an experienced stallion and mare, but a young stallion may find it a bit more difficult to figure out just what to do. I don't want to go into too much detail on the stallion side of things, because this book is about the breeding and raising of the foal, not about stud management (and if you don't know the basics of how babies are made, perhaps you should wait a while before breeding a foal!).

Just one thing I want to add, though, to hopefully save you from moments of panic if you're present at the covering. If you have a maiden

mare (one who has never been covered/bred before), please be aware that, like humans, horses have hymens so don't be shocked if your mare bleeds a bit after her first covering. (I didn't know this until just yesterday when one of my own mares was covered, and after a brief panic and a quick Google search, I found this out!)

After covering, the mare will be teased again and potentially covered again until she is out of estrus (the technical term for this is diestrus), at which point you then have to wait a couple of weeks before she can be checked by ultrasound to find out if she is pregnant (or you can be old-fashioned like me and just wait to see if she comes back into season!).

From this point onward the processes are the same whether the mare has been live covered or bred by AI, so let's take a quick look at AI now. AI, in case you were confusing it with artificial intelligence, means artificial insemination. This is clearly not the natural way of doing things, but it's very commonplace these days, sometimes for convenience or the ability to breed to a faraway stallion, sometimes just because the stallion owner wants to minimize the risk of injury or infection to their horse.

My strong recommendation, if you are considering AI, is that you first verify your foal will be eligible for registration with the appropriate body. It would be a shame if you bred a lovely foal but he/she was unable to be properly registered (we'll look at foal registration later). Something you must bear in mind if you own a Thoroughbred mare and are hoping to breed your own Thoroughbred racehorse: The Jockey Club *will not* accept registration of any foal conceived via non-natural route, which rules out AI as well as embryo transfer and cloning. Other breed registries may accept such non-traditionally bred foals. I did a quick Internet search and it appears that the Jockey Club is the only registry who do not permit AI at all. Some registries restrict it to, shall we say, freshly collected semen, but most permit the use of transported cooled semen, with fewer accepting the use of frozen semen.

The first step of the AI process is collection. This involves using a dummy mare (sometimes called a phantom), a fake, vaguely horse-shaped piece of equipment. An in-season mare may be brought to the area to help get the stallion aroused, but horses are smart creatures and a stallion experienced in use of the phantom will quickly learn why he's there and become sufficiently aroused without a mare being present. The procedure generally requires the involvement of at least two people in dealing with the stallion, one to handle the stallion, and one to do the actual collection. Obviously if a mare is being used she will also require her own handler. With a very experienced handler (and stallion) it may actually be possible to do the entire job single-handed, but as collection is an important and potentially dangerous task, I recommend that at least two people be involved.

After the stallion mounts the phantom, the attendant responsible for the actual collection will direct the stallion's penis into an artificial vagina (AV). The collection attendant will hold the AV close to the phantom to give the most natural position possible and will allow the stallion to thrust into it until he ejaculates. As the stallion then dismounts from the phantom, the attendant will carefully allow him to withdraw from the AV. It is important that the entire experience be kept as natural and pleasant as possible for the stallion, as clearly a stallion who finds the process uncomfortable or even painful will be far less interested in repeating the experience in rather the same way as a stallion who has been injured by a kicking mare may no longer find that mare quite so alluring.

Once the semen has been collected, it is taken to a laboratory to be processed, at which time it is generally incorporated with a semen extender, a liquid which preserves the viability of the sperm. (The need for such specialized on-site equipment is why some stallions are not offered for breeding via AI, or they will be transported from their home to a specialized facility for collection.) If the mare is on site, she will be inseminated immediately. If not, the semen will be stored in an incubator or warm water bath while the mare is prepared. If the semen is to be cooled for storage or shipping, an extender will *always* be used before the sample is slowly chilled. Equitainers are specially designed containers which can safely maintain the correct temperature (39–43°F/4–6°C) for up to forty-eight hours, which should be ample time to transport the semen to the mare. Due to this rather short timeframe, the mare must be at the optimum point in her estrus cycle when the sample is collected and shipped. Mares are generally inseminated just before ovulation (twelve to twenty-four hours before is the optimum time) so your vet must be heavily involved in this process to determine the best time for insemination. Many mare owners and vets find it easiest to have the mare board at the veterinary facility during this period to avoid unnecessary delays (and while you will therefore incur board charges, in all likelihood these will be the same or less than the cost of multiple vet visits). The other way semen can be prepared and stored is by freezing. From the mare owner's point of view, there isn't really much difference, though obviously the timeframe for use is a bit less stringent. The sperm is usually packaged in "straws" and these would be placed into a water bath to thaw gradually. This method definitely calls for your vet being involved.

The actual insemination method is the same whether the semen is fresh, cooled, or frozen. The mare will have her tail wrapped for cleanliness and is usually brought into an examination stock to protect the vet/AI tech from kicking. The mare's genital area will be thoroughly cleaned to minimize contamination. Using a gloved hand, the insemination pipette is inserted into the vagina. An insemination syringe connected to the pipette holds the semen. The pipette extends through the cervix, allowing the semen to be deposited directly into the uterus, then the semen is introduced slowly (to reduce the risk of damage). Once insemination is complete, the pipette is slowly removed. Some breeders may choose to inseminate the mare on two consecutive days, but if the insemination has been done correctly, at the correct time, this has been found to be unnecessary. In fact, the risk of uterine inflammation can make a repeat insemination more likely to cause problems than to enhance the chance of a successful outcome.

The final artificial breeding method sometimes used is embryo transfer. This is less commonly used due to high costs but it does allow for multiple foals from the same mare in a single year. It may be a preferable method in the case of a mare who, due to some injury, is not capable of carrying a foal to term. Some owners of high-performance mares may use this method so they can breed from the mare without losing any training or competition time. (As it sounds, embryo transfer tends to be about what the *owner* wants, not necessarily what is best for the horse!) An embryo transfer mare will be impregnated, either naturally or via AI, then the fertilized ovum is flushed from her uterus and placed into the uterus of another mare. This can be done surgically or non-surgically, but the surgical method has a higher success rate. Obviously, this should only be done by a qualified and experienced veterinary surgeon. The embryo will be flushed from the mare about seven days after fertilization, and this is done by flushing the uterus with a sterile saline solution, collecting the fluid as it exits the mare, and thus also collecting the embryo. The embryo will be examined under a microscope to verify suitability for the procedure, then either implanted into the recipient mare (if this is being done "fresh" then donor and recipient mares must have their estrus cycles synchronized) or potentially chilled and transported to wherever the recipient mare is. Foals resulting from this breeding method are genetically the offspring of the donor mare, in the same way that humans use a surrogate to carry a baby to term. Again, the acceptability of an embryo transfer foal by a breed registry should be checked *before* this is done or you will have carried out a costly procedure for a foal which cannot be registered.

Caslick/Pouret Operations

If your mare has undergone either of these surgical procedures, I recommend having more experienced help present at (or close to) foaling time. Caslick and Pouret surgeries are procedures which may be performed in mares with poor vulval conformation. The external vulval lips are the first line of defense in ensuring the vulval seal prevents feces, etc. from entering the reproductive tract. Some affected mares may also "windsuck," drawing air into the vagina, which also presents infection risk. Some mares have inherently poor conformation in this area, while in others the problem may be caused by age or poor body condition. In some cases, the issue has been caused due to poor condition, so all that may be required is to improve the mare's condition and body fat level (this problem is often evident in high performing mares where the muscle mass developed has caused body fat to be reduced below optimum levels).

If poor conformation is inherited, the most commonly used surgical treatment is a Caslick[1] operation. Briefly, this involves the mare being sedated and also a local anesthetic being administered to the exterior of the vulva. A narrow strip of skin is removed from the upper part of each side of the vulva and the two exposed areas are then sutured

---

1 Named for the veterinarian who first introduced the procedure in 1937, E. A. Caslick, DVM.

together. The purpose of this surgery is to reestablish the vulval seal, with the essential object being to close the vulval opening to level with the brim of the pelvis. The area heals within a week or so after the operation. It is vitally important that a mare who has undergone this procedure is "opened up" prior to foaling. Some breeders are comfortable to do this themselves once the mare is in second stage labor, simply using a pair of straight scissors. The vulva becomes numb during the foaling process, so this is often easily and safely done. However, if you plan to foal a Caslicked mare yourself, I recommend your vet open the mare a few days prior to her due date (in this instance a local anesthetic is often used). A Caslicked mare who is not opened up prior to foaling can suffer terrible injuries (even including the foal's feet penetrating the roof of the vagina so they enter the rectum and appear from the anus) which may be another good reason to open her a few days ahead of her due date. Of course, mares may foal when not at all expected, and this is always a risk in this situation.

A similar surgery, especially performed on older mares, is Pouret[2] surgery. The Pouret procedure is more radical than the Caslick operation, and is performed under a combination of spinal and local anesthesia. In this procedure, a dissection is made between the rectum and the roof of the vagina, freeing the vulva from the pull exerted by the rectum (whether due to age or poor conformation). The vulva is then able to return to a natural vertical alignment. The Pouret operation is generally only carried out in cases of severe malformation, however it should be noted that over time the effect may be reversed due to natural tissue contraction. The Pouret operation does not require the mare to be opened up prior to foaling.

In Season/Heat/Estrus

These are interchangeable terms, and you'll find that I tend to drift between all three! Mares are "in heat" or receptive to the advances of

---

2 Pouret surgery was introduced in 1982 and is named for the French veterinarian who introduced it, Dr. Edouard Pouret.

the stallion for just a few days per cycle, so when planning to send your mare off to be bred you need to start paying close attention to when she is in heat. Their heat cycles are linked to hours of daylight, which is why commercial breeding operations will often use artificial lighting to encourage mares to start coming into heat earlier in the year, since they ideally want the foals born as early in the year as possible. This is because bigger operations are generally producing foals for racing or show lives, and since racehorses all have an official birthday of January 1st, a foal which is born in July may end up racing against one born in January, which will always be six months older and more mature. The same goes for foals which are destined for the show ring as foals.

Mares have a twenty-one-day cycle, and are *generally* in heat for around five days and out for around sixteen. A longer heat (estrus) will mean a shorter time out of heat (diestrus). Early in the breeding season the mare could be in estrus for up to eight days, so her diestrus will be only thirteen days. At other times she may only be in estrus for two to three days. Regardless of the length of estrus/diestrus, the overall cycle does remain constant at twenty-one-days. When she is in estrus, the mare will display signs of being receptive, even if there is no stallion around. This can include repeatedly urinating in front of geldings (accompanied by "winking") and basically trying to make it clear that she is "in the mood." Some mares are pretty subtle about it. Mine are anything but!

So, with all contract arrangements in place, once I had a pretty good handle on Moyie's heat cycle, we scheduled her trip to see her new boyfriend. (Or boy toy really, since she was sixteen years his senior at that time). We got her ready to travel, with her padded boots and her snazzy leather helmet, then loaded her up for the trip. (A hint for traveling with any horse: if you use the leather helmet style poll guard as I do, it's really helpful if you can put two halters on your horse, a regular one, then the helmeted one over that. Use a leather or breakaway with the helmet, then use that one to secure the horse in the trailer. That way, when you get where you're going you can just pull off the over-halter to take off the helmet without having to try to unthread it from the headpiece of the halter.) Some stallion owners will provide mares with hay at an additional cost, but as we were obviously driving a truck and trailer up there anyway, it made just as much sense to take hay from home since Moyie's digestive system was accustomed to it. Pre-mixing her morning and evening feeds simply made life easier for both Amber and me as all she had to do was soak the evening feeds for an hour or so (she gets beet pulp and alfalfa cubes with her night grain) before feeding. *Then* we loaded her into the trailer and set off on the hour-plus journey north.

On arriving, the first thing I did was unload Moyie and take off her protective boots, etc., then I took her to her private paddock. I liked that Amber kept each mare in her own space. This helps minimize kicking, etc. I dumped Moyie's remaining hay on the ground in the paddock, and with that in front of her she no longer cared about me (she's very sentimental that way!). Then, we got to meet Outlaw and a couple of his foals from that year's crop, and both he and the foals confirmed what a good choice we'd made. When a stallion during breeding season can be led out of his stall on a halter and rope while mares (particularly my darling shrinking violet) are screaming for his attention, and he stands quietly by his owner while we chat . . . yes, that's a very good-natured stallion! He is an impressively built horse, but his temperament really shines through as one of his very best features. While I was admiring Moyie's new man, my wonderful husband had hauled all the hay and grain through to Amber's storage barn, then he also met Outlaw and approved wholeheartedly.

After stalling as long as we could, we had to leave, and leaving Moyie behind with someone who was practically a stranger was incredibly hard, especially since the last time she wasn't under my own care, she ended up so severely neglected. But Amber's care would prove to be every bit as thorough as mine, and she even sent me daily pictures of my baby because she knows how horse-mommies worry about their babies!

Now, of course Moyie decided to play hard to get, and she wouldn't come into heat to allow Outlaw to cover her. By the end of the week, she still hadn't been covered, so we made another trip up to Amber's, taking more hay and grain to keep Moyie going another few days. Maybe she was missing me (no, I know it's not likely!) but she did finally accept Outlaw's advances and was covered successfully. Once the deed was done, we headed back up with the trailer to collect our hopefully pregnant mare.

The easiest (and cheapest!) way to tell if a mare is actually pregnant is to wait and see if she comes into heat again. And guess what? Moyie did. Remember how I said they are generally in heat for about five days? Moyie came back into heat for one day. Which is just weird. I consulted with a friend who is a vet in Scotland and she confirmed that, yes, that was weird, so I called my vet here in Florida to come out and take a look to see if we could figure out what was going on. Our vet carried out an ultrasound examination to check if Moyie was indeed pregnant or, if not, what was happening in there. If you haven't seen a mare getting an ultrasound before, it involves long gloves and the vet sticking an ultrasound probe into the mare's rectum to get a picture from the uterus. Unlike women, horses cannot get an ultrasound examination through the stomach as the uterus lies buried behind too many other things. The ultrasound showed that, no, she was not pregnant (darn it!) but that she had a very large follicle. I'm trying really hard to not get too technical with this, but basically the ovary produces a follicle which grows/swells, then delivers an egg for fertilization. That is an enormous oversimplification, but it should be enough for our purposes here. Moyie had a very large follicle, which meant that she was going to ovulate in the next day or so.

Just to be thorough, our vet also decided to do a cervical examination on Moyie, to be doubly sure that everything was as it should be. This is a great example of her steady temperament, as he performed a

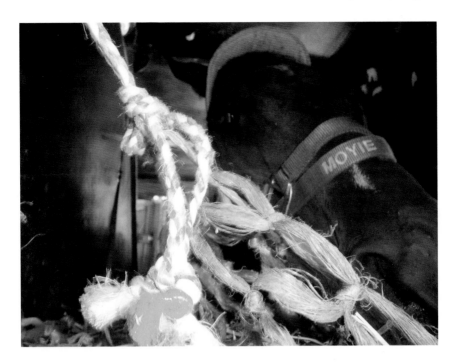

cervical exam (requiring a fresh long glove and some lubrication on his arm) without her being sedated. She simply stood in the barn aisle on a halter and loose lead rope while he gave her a thorough examination (even the vet was pretty surprised). Long story short, everything in there was perfect so she was ready to ovulate and should be coming in heat almost immediately. I called Amber and told her the situation then, you guessed it, Moyie was back to her boots and helmet and trailer ride. I took her back to Amber's, knowing she was ready to ovulate and be covered. But guess what? She still wasn't in heat. Whether due to the time of year (a lot of mares were having difficult-to-pinpoint cycles that year) or her age, or her just wanting another visit with Outlaw, Moyie's ovulation and heat cycles were out of sync. When she was in heat, there was no egg. When there was an egg, she wasn't coming in heat (another huge oversimplification).

This time though, Amber was taking one of her other horses to see her vet, so she loaded up Moyie and took her along. The vet checked and confirmed her ovulation status, so gave her a shot of something that would bring her into heat. I think it was just that same afternoon that Moyie was very definitely in heat and more than receptive to Outlaw's advances, so Outlaw covered her, then again the next day, and then she lost interest (which often means they are now pregnant so have no more use for the stallion—mares are fickle that way!). With fingers, toes, and eyes crossed, we collected Moyie and brought her home to wait and see if she was indeed pregnant. And so began some *very* long months.

Chapter 3

The Long Road

The length of an average equine pregnancy is 340 days, but anything from 320 to 370 is considered "normal." It's not unheard of for a mare to deliver a healthy foal after a gestation period of 399 days! Generally speaking, any foal born before 320 days is considered premature, but a foal born at 300 days or earlier has a very poor chance of survival, around 10 percent.

Fun fact: Despite the fact that the word trimester means three months, and last time I checked three times three was nine, people still refer to a mare's pregnancy as having three trimesters! In the case of horses, though, the trimesters are defined as:

- First trimester: Day 0–113
- Second trimester: Day 114–225
- Third trimester: Day 226–foaling

First Trimester (0–113 Days)

Now, many people these days with the rise of technology opt for their mare to get an ultrasound exam not only to confirm pregnancy but also to check for the presence of twin embryos. While it is possible for a mare to successfully carry twin foals, it really isn't advisable as there is a high likelihood of things going wrong. A foal at birth is a relatively huge animal, so having two in there really is something to be avoided. With twins, you could lose both foals, or lose one quite late in the pregnancy, causing problems with the survivor. You could also lose your mare. If

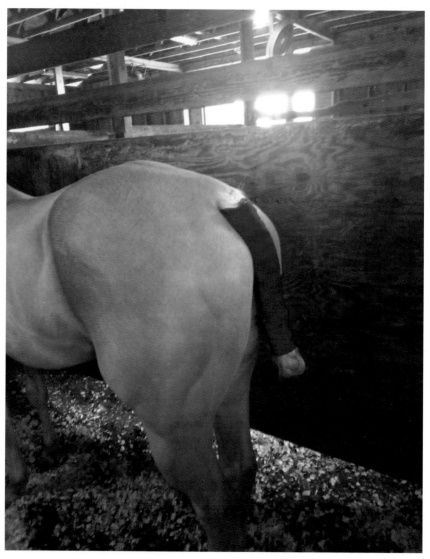

It makes your vet's life a little easier if you wrap your mare's tail before the ultrasound is carried out. I like to braid it, fold it up, then wrap it neatly so it looks rather like a polo pony's tail.

the mare is able to successfully bring both to term, you could have a healthy foal and a weakling—think of the runt of the litter—or two rather poorly foals. The effort of delivering twins could also potentially be too much for the mare, and if she makes it through that, she could struggle to produce enough milk to feed two hungry babies! For this reason, a vet will generally check this between day fourteen and sixteen of confirmed pregnancy. Up until this point, the embryos are sort of free floating in the uterus and haven't yet attached themselves. It sounds a bit nasty, but if twins are detected, the vet will simply "pinch one off." This is pretty much just what it sounds like. Because the ultrasound is performed rectally, the vet already has their hand in position close to the embryos, so they simply crush one of them to prevent it from developing further. I know this sounds awful, but it is quite commonly done and is considered to be the best course of action if twin embryos are detected before they attach themselves to the uterine wall.

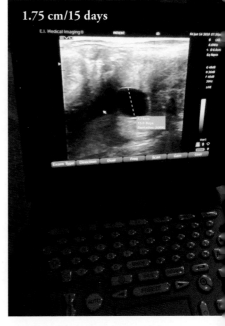

1.75 cm/15 days

With all of that said, I chose not to ultrasound Moyie. My main reasoning was that we would *not* be trying again if she wasn't pregnant. I knew there was always a risk of twins, but I also knew that she had no history of twins *and* when my vet had performed an ultrasound before, there was only *one* follicle, which meant one egg. Twin foals are most often from separate eggs, not from the splitting of a single egg, so her chances of twins were extremely low. Choosing not to ultrasound is very definitely something each mare owner should decide carefully. Something else to consider is that not having a pregnancy confirmed via ultrasound may invalidate any foal guarantee within your breeding contract with the

Modern ultrasound is very informative. As you can see, this can even estimate how far along the mare is by the size of the conceptus (not even a fetus yet!)

stallion owner. I did, however, have a vet coming out to our property a few weeks after her return from stud (he is also a wonderful chiropractor and was coming to treat another horse) so asked him to take a look at Moyie while he was there. After a brief examination (no ultrasound), he confirmed my belief that she was indeed pregnant. Yay!

For the first half to two thirds of the pregnancy, the foal is being built. The latter part of pregnancy is when this little miniature foal grows to its full foaling size (from around day 250, the foal will gain around one pound per day!), and this is the part of pregnancy when your mare will need additional nutrition. So, for the first trimester, Moyie's life didn't need to change at all. Science has allowed us to have a pretty good idea of how big the embryo/fetus is at various stages (it is an embryo until day fifty-five of pregnancy, then becomes known as a fetus). There are some accepted comparisons which will be shown as we move forward to give you a bit of an idea of how big baby is getting as we go along.

Nine days after successful insemination, the embryo is microscopic, the size of a pinpoint, and weighs a whopping 3/2000 of an ounce! Owners will often have a second ultrasound carried out between days forty-five to sixty, to confirm that there is a heartbeat and that all appears to be going as it should.

Day 40: the embryo is around three-quarters of an inch from crown to rump and weighs just under half an ounce.

There are some additional veterinary type requirements for the pregnant mare, and the most important of these is the administration of additional vaccinations against EHV-1, Equine Herpesvirus 1 (also known as rhino). This virus is believed to possibly induce abortion in a pregnant mare, and while Moyie was not going to be traveling or in contact with any unvaccinated horses, I wasn't going to take the risk of *not* vaccinating her and potentially losing the foal to something I could have easily prevented. If you have your vet come out to administer the vaccinations, this will be a bit more expensive, but I already give my own horses their shots myself, so adding a couple more for Moyie wasn't a huge deal. There are a couple of available EHV-1 vaccines which you can order online or pick up at your local feed store (I got mine at Tractor Supply). They aren't terribly expensive to purchase, so if you're already giving shots to your horse (and she's equally okay about getting shots!) then it's not going to be terribly pricey to do. Anyway, your mare will require her regular shots too, so if you time it right you will only have to add two extras as she needs the EHV-1 at three, five, seven, and nine months gestation. Yes, of course it's entirely possible that everything would have been perfectly fine without those extra shots, but I would hate to have decided against the extras and then have her lose the foal. Regardless of the actual reason, I would always blame myself for not giving the shots. The first of these extra shots is due during the first trimester, around day ninety of pregnancy. The other sort of veterinary thing that needs to be done in this time period (at least in the sixty to ninety day range) is to deworm your mare. She should be given whichever dewormer she is due for (assuming that you are following a traditional program of rotating different chemicals to minimize the chances of immunity).

Day 60: the fetus is now two-and-a-half inches long and weighs around one ounce.

Day 100: in the last forty days the fetus has grown considerably, now around seven inches long and weighing one pound

Second Trimester (114–225 Days)

We need to administer our EHV-1 vaccine two more times in this trimester. The first should be given at day 150 or around that day for

Day 150: twelve inches long, six pounds.

full benefit. At this time, you should also deworm your mare with the next chemical on your regular rotation. Our second EHV-1 vaccine this trimester should be given at day 210.

Moyie was healthy and happy during her first two trimesters. She was growing a belly, which was certainly a big comfort to me if not to her, and everything seemed to be progressing on schedule. Apparently, Moyie had read the same foaling book I had, because she was literally textbook. I continued to ride her lightly and use her for the occasional kid's riding lesson, until the point where she was clearly unhappy about being saddled. Now, one of Moyie's issues has always been that she has poor feet, and particularly her right front is extremely flat and shallow (at times the hoof wall from coronet to ground has been just over two inches!). There are plenty of anecdotes from pregnant women about how their hair and nails have grown wonderfully long and healthy during pregnancy, and I was thrilled to see that Moyie was having the same reaction to her pregnancy hormones. When we first consid-

ered breeding her, our farrier at the time had said that she may require front shoes if pregnant to offer additional support and protection to her feet. As it turned out, her hooves grew much better while she was pregnant, and by the time she foaled she had as close to a "normal horse" right

What a difference a few weeks makes!

Day 180: nineteen inches long, twenty-five pounds.

front as I've ever seen on her (it did revert to poorer growth after foaling, but I have to say that it is still definitely better than pre-pregnancy even now more than three years later).

She very definitely bloomed while pregnant and only toward the very end did she start to seem uncomfortable as the foal became more active and *much* bigger! As you can imagine, there's not a whole lot of room in there for a foal in the later stages of growth, and it's quite fascinating (and a little unnerving) to be able to see the movements of the foal through the mare's flanks. Especially cool when you find that if you rub/push in the right area at the right time, the foal will kick back against you!

Third Trimester (226–340 Days)

The final EHV-1 vaccination should be given at 270 days (roughly nine months). Now, to be honest, I delayed Moyie's nine-month shot by a couple of weeks, giving it around her 300th day of pregnancy. Why? Well, you want to give your mare her regular booster shots around four to six weeks before foaling to stimulate her immune system to produce the necessary antibodies, because those antibodies will then be

Day 270: twenty-seven inches long, seventy to eighty pounds.

contained within the colostrum, that all-important first milk. In that way, the immunity is passed along to the foal. By administering Moyie's boosters when I did, that shot covered both the EHV-1 *and* immunity boosting requirement all in one. The shot I gave Moyie was her usual six-monthly combination vaccine, covering EHV-1 and EHV-4 (also sometimes called "rhino," because the EHV stands for Equine Herpesvirus and this can cause *Rhino*pneumonitis), EET and WEE (Eastern and Western Equine Encephalomyelitis), Tetanus, Influenza, and West Nile Virus. I recommend discussing vaccination plans with your vet (especially if you administer your own vaccines) to ensure your mare and foal are given the best possible chance of adequate protection. Vaccine requirements also vary between states/countries, so your mare may need more or less than Moyie received, depending on where you are located.

Around day 300 you should deworm the mare again, using whichever dewormer is next on your rotation. If you have a Caslicked mare and you are *not* comfortable opening her yourself at foaling time, you should arrange to have your vet open her up. If your vet is giving the vaccinations, you could probably combine the two procedures in one visit. Now is also the time to move your mare to the intended foaling area (if necessary) to allow her to get comfortable in the new surroundings. If she is going to move any significant distance, moving now will also let her body get acclimated to any different bugs, etc. in the area so she can build some immunity and therefore pass it to the foal. It may be necessary to move your mare a bit earlier, at least thirty days before her due date, but preferably around ninety days before, due to the problems associated with a type of grass called Tall Fescue.

Equine Fescue Toxicosis[1]

It's quite valuable to understand just why *Acremonium coenophialum* can be such an issue. Yeah, I know. Acre . . . what? Acremonium coenophialum is a fungus, specifically an endophytic fungus, which can be found on a type of grass called tall fescue. The best way to check if your pasture is indeed tall fescue would be to take a sample of the grass and have it identified, because if your pasture does not contain tall fescue, you could probably skip the rest of this section (unless of course you're really interested). If your pasture *does* contain tall fescue, you should send samples for testing to find out whether it is infested with this endophyte fungus. For both the grass identification and endophyte testing, your best first port of call is your local agriculture department or extension office. If you don't already know where that is, just ask Google, or Bing, or whatever your preferred search engine may be.

Let's say that you have had your pasture tested and it does indeed contain endophyte infested tall fescue. Well, first of all, while this does have some pretty serious implications for a pregnant mare, it's not something you need to *panic* about. The simplest remedy for this situation is to move your mare off the infected pasture around ninety days prior to her due date. This allows ample time for the effects of the endophyte to leave her system, thereby removing the issue.

---

1 REFERENCE: "Equine fescue toxicosis: signs and symptoms," D.L. Cross, L.M. Redmond, J.R. Strickland, *Journal of Animal Science* 1995. 73:899–908.

But, what does this fungus actually do to the mare? Studies on the effects on pregnant mares grazing affected tall fescue record the following problems:

- Increased gestation period: The hormones that prepare the mare's body to give birth are called progestogens (the major one of these is progesterone). Mares affected by equine fescue toxicosis have decreased levels of progestogens, meaning that the mare's body is not stimulated to make the necessary changes for birth at the appropriate time. This leads to the marked increase in gestation length (an average of twenty-seven days has been recorded).

- Dystocia (difficult birth): When the reproductive tract is not sufficiently prepared for the foaling process, prolonged gestation can result in a foal's skeletal size being greater than normal, or in fetal malpresentation (the foal can be rotated 90° to 180° from a normal delivery position).

- Stillbirths: 50 percent of all mares on affected pasture delivered dead foals. Failure of the mare or foal to initiate events to promote normal birth can have catastrophic outcomes including death of the foal or even death of the mare.

- Agalactia (failure to produce milk): This occurred in 100 percent of affected mares. Prolactin stimulates the mare's body to begin producing milk, but decreased levels of prolactin are seen in affected mares, along with estrogen, which is elevated from normal levels.

- Placental retention: Affected mares show a five times greater incidence of retained placenta (we'll cover the problems this causes a bit later). The opposite may also occur, with premature placental separation at foaling, causing what is known as a "red bag" foaling.

- Increased placental weight, thickness, and toughness.

- Decreased prolactin and progesterone; increased estrogen.

- Increased sweating due to elevated body temperature.

So, what can be done? There have been a few different studies carried out, including feeding a greater concentration of grain (specifically cracked corn), selenium supplementation, and various drug therapies. One drug, Domperidone, given either orally for thirty days prior to a mare's due date or by subcutaneous injection for ten days prior to her due date, was shown to give almost complete recovery from symptoms. Other drugs, dopamine antagonists, etc. were deemed to have too many potential secondary neuroleptic side effects to be considered viable treatment options. As mentioned before, the simplest form of treatment is to move the mare off the affected pasture, either moving her to a pasture which is known to be free of tall fescue or moving her off pasture entirely. Mares who were moved ten to twenty days prior to foaling still experienced greater than average agalactia. Mares moved thirty days before had normal births and lactation, but still showed an increased incidence of placental retention. Mares moved earlier than thirty days prior to due date showed a total recovery from symptoms. The rule of thumb seems to be that if you *do* need to move your mare from an infected pasture, ninety days before due date is a sensible time to do it, just to be safe.

Chapter 4

Getting Ready for the Big Day

Preparing for Foaling

One of the major things we had to do in preparation for foaling was to create a foaling stall in our barn. We dismantled the wall between two of the stalls to open up the space, but because our barn has dirt floors instead of concrete, our stalls have differing floor levels, so we had to haul down many wheelbarrow loads of earth (actually we used rotted-down muckheap, because that is basically no longer manure but just good topsoil) to equalize the floors. Once the floors were level, the whole stall was thoroughly pressure-washed and allowed to dry before we put in fresh bedding and introduced Moyie to her new home. We did this a month or so before the foal was due, partly in case of an early arrival but mostly because that was when we had the time to do it. Moyie of course was delighted with her upgrade from a standard bedroom to a suite, and she wasted no time in making herself at home (i.e. rolling in the fresh shavings until she looked like a very large, rather fat sugared donut).

When you are making these preparations, whether your mare is intended to foal in a stall or outdoors, make sure that all walls/fences, etc. are sturdy and safe with no sharp objects (like nail heads/ends) sticking out which could injure either mare or foal. You could use a mild disinfectant solution to clean down the walls, but we felt that pressure washing was sufficient, and since Moyie was used to her stall (even though it was getting a bit bigger), she was already accustomed to any bugs that may be present. As an aside, I always feel that horses *and* people need to be exposed to bugs to build immunity. I think this is why some people get sick a lot more, because they're constantly disinfecting and sanitizing, so they never develop immunity!

Around this time you should also prepare all the necessities for foaling time. There are foaling kits available from online veterinary catalogs, and I looked at one which contained iodine and gloves and skin wash and tail wrap and special soap and a time sheet (to note down what is happening when) and a bag for the placenta and string . . . and then I got in touch with Amber to find out what she recommended. She said she has iodine for the umbilical cord, a large garbage bag for the placenta and, yeah, that's about all that's needed, so I relaxed my plans a bit and just made sure I had the usual first aid type stuff. Of course, this applies to a normal, straightforward, complication-free foaling. If your first foal is anything other than "normal," *call the vet!* If you don't like touching icky stuff, a couple pairs of latex exam gloves won't hurt. It's also not a bad idea to have a couple of old towels on hand, in case you need to help the mare dry the foal or even just for drying off your own hands. It seemed like I was constantly washing and drying my hands when Moyie foaled. The other thing I purchased in the months leading up to foaling was a foal slip, or foal halter. Actually, my mom bought it, because she "wanted to get something for the baby," so I guess that was Moyie's baby shower gift! My preference was for a leather one, as they will more easily break if the foal gets hung up on something, and I found a lovely traditional style foal halter online for just under $20. They also have a short leather strap attached, about a foot long, to give you something to catch hold of more easily. Obviously waiting until your mare is in labor to think about getting a halter for the foal isn't a good plan! Something else you may want to consider, depending on where you are located, is the possibility of it being very cold when the foal is born. Or at least very cold from the point of view of a newborn whose last eleven months or so have been spent in a perfectly heated environment. Foal blankets aren't terribly expensive. I definitely suggest going for the cheapest option as it will be outgrown pretty quickly unless you plan to breed a lot of foals over the years.

By this point in time, Moyie's feed intake had also increased quite substantially. I hesitate to give any advice on this subject as all mares will be different, but your mare should look healthy, neither underweight nor overly fat. If your mare is eating a diet which she's happy and healthy on, I recommend simply increasing it, but if

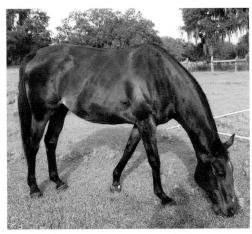

Six months in foal.

you choose to change *what* you are feeding, remember to do it gradually. If you look on the grain bag you'll find recommended feeding weights for various different stages of life and work. As an example, the feed I use recommends that a horse at maintenance (i.e. not working) should receive 0.2 to 0.5 pounds of grain per one hundred pounds of bodyweight. So, a one-thousand-pound horse would be given between two and five pounds of grain per day, and a mare in her first two trimesters needs the same. In her last trimester this increases from 0.5 to 0.75 pounds of grain per one hundred pounds of bodyweight. In early lactation (after the foal is born and the mare is producing milk), she would need 1 to 1.5 pounds per one hundred pounds, so between ten and fifteen pounds per day, as milk production uses a lot of calories. Unless your vet recommends pregnancy/pre-foaling supplements, your mare (and foal) should be getting all the nutrients they need from a good, balanced diet. As your mare gets further along toward the end of her pregnancy, don't be surprised if she seems to take a little longer to eat her food—her intestines are losing space to the foal!

The best place for your pregnant mare to be is (weather permitting) out at pasture. If you are in a colder climate, you may have limited access during the winter months, or the weather may be too bad for you to let your mare out very much, but I do think that being able to move around naturally is the best thing (for any horse, but especially a pregnant mare) so the more space you are able to allow her the better. Of course, the flip side of having her turned out is that it's harder to monitor her and watch for signs of foaling. There are a number of ways to remotely monitor your mare for signs of labor, such as transmitters which attach to the halter or are even strapped around the mare's body, sending data to either a receiver unit or directly to your phone. These items are generally quite costly (at least a few hundred dollars) and often rely on line of sight for best range, which means that if your mare is in the barn or far off in the field, signal may not be good. The other monitoring method is, of course, the old-fashioned way: sitting up late and watching! If you have security cameras in your barn, you can sit in the comfort of your home and watch the cameras rather than sitting out in the barn. Also, some mares will not foal unless they are alone, so sitting in the barn may make her delay foaling (yes, they can do this!).

Before you start losing sleep, there are some early warning signs to look out for, which normally indicate that your mare is getting ready to foal in the next day or two. Hopefully your mare will be one of the kind ones (like Moyie) who follows the textbook list of pre-foaling indicators, because some mares like to show no signs at all until you go out to the barn one morning and find four extra hooves on the ground! The first is how long she's been pregnant. I started doing late night physical checks on Moyie (as well as just checking in on her stall camera) about a month before her due date. These checks were very cursory; right before my own bedtime I would pop out to the barn and just look her over, usually without even going into the stall. I felt that, as well as actually checking on her, it also meant she had time to get accustomed to me just popping in at night, so it wouldn't disturb or upset her if she were in labor. (It also got the other horses in the barn used to it, so they didn't make a fuss when I appeared late at night.) So what was I looking for?

Signs to Watch For

Around six weeks before foaling, your mare will start to produce milk, so you will see her udder getting fatter (known as "bagging up") as it fills. Don't be concerned if the udder seems to stop swelling or get smaller at times. This is completely normal. Like everything else, though, some mares will have big udders (some literally dripping milk) for weeks before birth while others will barely even start bagging up before the

foal arrives. If your mare has had a foal in the past, it can be useful to find out from the previous owner (if possible) whether she showed good signs or not. In our case, Moyie's last known foal had been quite some time in the past (I think fifteen/sixteen years, unless there were others which were not registered) so getting in touch with her owner at that time wasn't an option, partly because she would probably have foaled at a barn without the owner present, and partly because even if I could have tracked down someone who *was* there, the chances of them remembering any specifics from one horse so long ago were pretty slim.

You will also notice the belly change shape, going from being very fat side-to-side to dropping to a much lower underline. This is completely normal as the foal is repositioning itself in preparation for birth. Throughout most of the pregnancy, the foal can be visualized as lying on its back kind of curled up like the world's biggest shrimp. In preparation for birth, the foal will reposition itself to lie on its front with both forelegs extended and the nose neatly lined up on top of the legs (in a correct foaling position). This generally happens a week before foaling, and the shape change in the mare is usually quite obvious.

The mare may also develop some edema under her belly in late pregnancy. This is related to the production of milk as the veins supplying the udder become more visibly distended. This is usually nothing to worry about, but if you are concerned at the extent of edema, I suggest contacting your vet. It's not common, but it is possible for the abdominal muscles and pre-pubic tendon which support the uterus to become damaged or even rupture, removing the support structure which holds the foal in place. This instance requires immediate veterinary attention for the safety of both mare and foal. The other place you may notice a shape change is around the mare's hindquarters, as the muscles around the pelvis relax in preparation for the foal passing through. This starts to happen a couple of weeks before foaling.

Moyie developed a small amount of edema, but nothing which was concerning at all (here she is 347 days pregnant . . . yes, seven days past her due date!).

After a few weeks of my nightly checks on Moyie, I switched from simply taking a quick look at her over the door/wall (our stalls have half-height front walls) to actually going into the stall and checking her a bit more closely. Nothing too difficult, a look at her udder to see if it was much bigger than last time I'd looked, a bit of a poke and prod (or palpation, if you want to be fancy) at her hindquarters to see if the muscles were soft, and just a general assessment of her demeanor to see if she was agitated. I also began checking if she'd eaten all her feed, as going off food can be an early sign of first stage labor.

The pH level of the mare's milk can help you predict if foaling should be expected in the next twelve hours or so. Testing for this involves milking a few drops from her udder and using pH test strips to check the levels. The milk will be at a pH of above seven prior to foaling, but as she gets closer to foaling time, the pH level will drop. Most mares will foal within a matter of hours to a day after the pH has dropped to 6.8 or less. You can buy pH testing kits specifically for pre-foaling checks. Some of these are a bit complicated, requiring the milk to be mixed in specific amounts with distilled water, etc. as they also check calcium levels. The mare's milk will also start to change color when she is closer to foaling. It will shift from a clear-ish color to looking like, well, milk! I guess I should also explain just how to get the milk. Moyie, being the sweet girl that she is, had absolutely no problems with me messing with her udder. Your own mare may have different ideas, so please be careful! If you've ever milked a cow, it's the same process. Think of how a foal or calf gets the milk out. They take the teat in their mouth (it's okay, you can use your fingers!) and sort of push up toward the udder, then clamp down a bit and pull to get the milk flowing. If your mare is okay with you doing it, you'll get the hang of it pretty easily. As well as the milk becoming milky looking, before foaling it also becomes sweeter tasting (I guess it's the colostrum building up in it). Yes, I went there. In the last week or so before foaling date, I would milk out a drop or two and taste it. Your own comfort level with doing that may differ from mine, but I don't see it as any different from cow's milk (plus, in many ancient cultures they routinely drank mare's milk or made cheese from it, so what's the big deal?). But, whether you choose cheap pH strips or expensive ones, or any other method of checking, please do be careful not to get kicked.

Closer to foaling time, maybe the day of, you will see some other warning signs. The teats of the udder will fill as birth approaches, and "wax up." This is just a little waxy looking buildup which forms on the tips of the teats as a small amount of colostrum escapes and dries on the skin. Some mares may actually drip/run milk instead which, while sort of helpful as a guide, can be a problem because the all-important colostrum is in the early part of the milk. Colostrum is a substance contained within the mare's milk, and it contains huge amounts of antibodies, which is why it is vital that the foal is able to suckle from the mare as soon as possible. If the mare has run milk, or if for some other reason there is doubt as to the quality of colostrum, then alternatives may be needed, but this is something we'll touch on again after we get past the actual giving birth part.

I continued my nightly checks on Moyie all the way to her due date of May 6th, day 340 after she was successfully bred. Then, I continued on May 7th, 8th, 9th . . . yep, this was the one part of her pregnancy which was not textbook. The evening of May 12th I was 99 percent

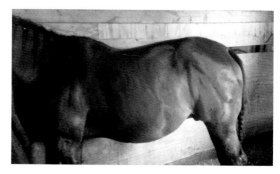

sure that she was showing signs of first stage labor, and her belly had changed shape that day, so I kept a close watch on her for most of the night. She was lightly sweating and clearly uncomfortable, pacing and rolling in her stall.

May 12th, 2016

This went on for hours to the point where I decided to bake a batch of cookies while I waited, just to keep myself semi-sane. (Maybe I'll put the cookie recipe in an appendix in case you want to do the same!) And then, finally it happened. She settled down and went to sleep. Apparently she wasn't quite ready to give that baby up.

Foaling Process

On May 15th, Moyie was definitely out of sorts when I fed her at night. When I checked on her later that night, she was slightly sweaty, waxed up, and the muscles around the top of her tail were very soft indeed. Also (yet another example of how intimate you get with your mare in this process) her vulva was very relaxed, sort of puffy and droopy, and the mucus membrane on the inside was a deep red instead of the usual salmon pink. As you can see, her udder was also *very* full by now (it gets quite shiny as it fills),

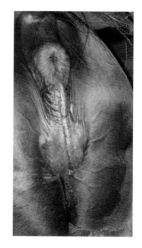

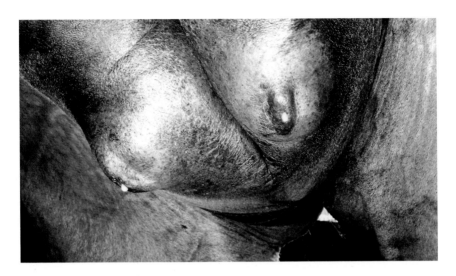

and she was literally dripping milk, all very clear indicators that she *should* foal very, very soon. With this in mind, and as she was still quite calm about the whole thing, I quickly braided her tail and folded it up, then wrapped the entire tail with a cohesive bandage. Then, I put her halter on (better doing that now than when she's agitated), made sure her stall was clean, and left her to get on with things. Well, I actually went into the house, started a pot of coffee, and made myself comfortable in front of the camera monitor with a book. I went back out to the barn around midnight, mostly because Moyie looked *very* sweaty, but it appeared that she had just managed to lie down in a pee spot in her stall (she likes to do that!). I guess it was around one-thirty or two in the morning that I was sure that we were on for tonight, as she was becoming more agitated. I threw on some barn clothes and shoes (make sure that whatever you wear for foaling is something you don't mind possibly getting ruined!), glanced at the camera again, then went back to the bedroom to tell hubby that the foal was on its way *now* as I could see the white "bag" starting to show under Moyie's tail.

The bag, technically called the amnion, signals that the mare is in second stage labor, which is the actual delivery of the foal. Moyie's bag was white, as it should be. If the membrane appears red in color, this is colloquially known as "red bag" and is *not* normal. The prospect of this situation was one which certainly frightened me, and it is why if you are foaling your mare at home you should either have a more experienced person assisting you or at least have your vet on call.

Moyie was now well into second stage labor. She would lie down, straining a bit, then get up and walk around before lying down and straining some more. The thinking is that this up and down and wandering around helps to maneuver the foal into the best position for delivery. From outside the stall, we were able to see two feet (one a bit ahead of the other, since this position puts the foal's shoulders at a slight angle, making it easier for them to pass through the mare's pelvis) and then a little nose lying on top of the legs. It was a huge relief to see that we had a normal foal presentation, so I could stop my fingers from hovering near my phone in case I needed to call my vet. Now, if at all possible, you should let your mare take care of things herself. Of course, watch her carefully, but in the vast majority of foalings, human intervention is not required. *With that said*, due to Moyie being an older mare (okay, and me being an ultra-nervous horse mommy), I decided to give her just a little bit of help. My decision was

Everything just where it should be.

partly because the amnion had been torn during Moyie's up-and-down antics, which meant that if the foal were to slip back inside her, there was risk of suffocation. This is why it's important for your mare to feel as comfortable as possible with you handling all parts of her. You don't want to stress her by invading her space at this time if she's not accustomed to you being up close and personal.

Moyie is extremely good tempered, and she also trusts me very much, so she was perfectly happy that I came into her stall to help out. Of course, when she lay down for the last time, she lay up close to the wall, which could have made things difficult as space was limited, but fortunately she lay with her back to the wall. Who knows, maybe she actually wanted the wall behind her to push against it. Anyway, I explained to my husband that I wasn't going to *pull* the foal out, but was simply going to help Moyie, so I took hold of both tiny, wet fetlocks, and when Moyie pushed I pulled a *tiny* bit, and when she relaxed I held the foal in place so it didn't slip back at all. If you *do* have to provide this kind of assistance (or even more forceful pulling in case of problems), make sure to pull the foal in a downward direction toward

the mare's hocks, as this mimics the natural direction of birth and is therefore both most effective *and* least likely to cause any damage to mare or foal.

After a fairly short time, let's say a few minutes, the foal's shoulders came through, and they were some *big* shoulders! Once the shoulders are out, the foal will *not* be slipping back in. Almost the second she felt the shoulders pass through, Moyie surprised me by getting to her feet and delivered the foal's body and hind legs! I made sure that the foal was breathing and that there were four feet, two eyes, two ears, and two nostrils (hey, this was my first foaling, I was excited!). Moyie getting to her feet had broken the umbilical cord, which may not have been optimal but certainly doesn't seem to have affected the foal's health. Hubby passed me the bottle of iodine I had outside the stall and I quickly sprayed the umbilical stump with that to ward off infections (some people use a little plastic cup and dip the stump in iodine, but the spray seemed much easier). Note: You must not use "neat" iodine as this is far too strong and would burn the tissue. The iodine commonly

We have a foal!

sold in feed stores and the like is usually a 2 percent concentration and this is fine.

At this point we both looked at the foal's belly and said it was a filly, and I texted the stallion owner (who is amazing at keeping in touch during pregnancy and foaling) to tell her Moyie had just produced a beautiful big filly. Now I know enough to realize that the umbilical stump (which is a few inches long) may obscure other things, and maybe instead of going by that I should have looked under the foal's tail to check gender. (In the simplest of terms, one hole means boy, two holes means girl!) But I didn't. So a few minutes later when the foal moved I had to send a second text saying "Oops, cord was in the way, it's a boy!"

Yes, Moyie had delivered us a gorgeous paint colt.

I had always been fairly confident that Moyie would be a good mother, but she surpassed all my expectations. She licked her new son dry, making the most beautiful little burbling sounds to him all the time. While she was doing this, I didn't interfere with their bonding, but I did have one other task to take care of. After foaling, the amnion/placenta is attached to the mare (this will be delivered in a little while, which is called third stage labor). You don't want the mare to stand on this, as this can pull it out before it is ready, potentially leaving pieces behind that can cause major problems. The standard practice is to take some string and tie the placenta up into a ball of sorts behind the mare, then just let it hang until nature takes its course. I had to retie it a couple of times to get it secure (trust me, the stuff is *slippery!*) but that was dealt with, I came out of the stall to give them some time together (and to hug my husband).

Generally speaking, if a foal hasn't managed to get to their feet within an hour of birth, there may be a problem. Moyie clearly knew exactly what was expected of her, and also what she expected of her son. She cleaned him all over while he probably tried to figure out why his world had suddenly gotten so big. After 350 days folded up inside his mom, even a foaling stall must have seemed huge. We have some beautiful photographs of Moyie tending to her baby, and also some of

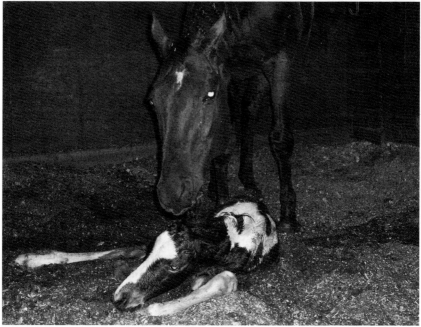

Got to get those ears clean!

him starting to get his suck reflex going as he's sucking his tongue. The other horses in the barn must have wondered what on earth was going on and why the humans kept going "Awww!" After maybe twenty to thirty minutes, when her baby didn't seem to be putting any real effort into getting up, Moyie got a bit more assertive in her suggestion that he should give it a try, and she would gently bite on his wither and almost try to lift him to his feet. After this happened a few times, he got the hint and started making some real efforts to get to his feet. As I'm sure you can imagine, there were quite a few false starts as he tried to get those impossibly long legs under control, and there were a few times he looked at his own legs like, "C'mon guys, help me out here!" When he finally did manage to get up on his feet, he almost immediately nose-dived onto the floor again, so he took a little break until Moyie suggested, strongly, that he try again.

Okay, son, time to get up.

While he was making these attempts, he would give the cutest little calls to Moyie. Sort of like underwater whinnies, but very clearly a newborn's sound. Our other horses were fascinated by this weird noise. I was back in Moyie's stall for most of this time, not doing anything, but just being there. I didn't want to affect their bonding, but I also wanted to be sure everything was okay, and that Moyie was okay with me being so close to her baby (in case anything went wrong and I did need to handle him). She was absolutely fine with my presence but, as I've said many times already, all mares are different so just be careful not to interfere with their bonding or get hurt if your mare is foal proud and doesn't want you near the newborn.

Sometimes a mare will reject her newly arrived foal, showing no interest in helping with cleaning the foal or allowing it to nurse when it does get to its feet. This must be dealt with carefully to avoid distressing either animal or having them injured. If the mare is simply unsure of this wet little stranger, it may be sufficient to just hold the mare on a halter while the foal is assisted to finding the udder. If she tries to kick the foal away, then the mare's front leg may be held up to make it difficult to kick (in this case I would probably hold the front leg on the side the foal is approaching). Often, once the foal has latched on and nursed, the mare will relax as she understands what is happening. If the mare does appear to be rejecting the foal, they must be closely monitored until you are sure she has accepted her baby. If she does not, you will be left in the same position as if your foal were an orphan (we'll cover this a little later). The ultimate level of rejection, though thankfully quite rare, would be a mare who savages her foal. This can cause serious injury or even death to the newborn (an acquaintance actually had a mare who deliberately trampled her foal to death). If you see the mare showing aggression to her foal, you *must* remove the foal and restrain the mare. It is possible that aggression is simply due to discomfort, and sometimes if the mare is suitably restrained to allow the foal to nurse, thus alleviating pressure in the udder, she will become less aggressive as she accepts the foal. But if you do observe any kind of aggressive

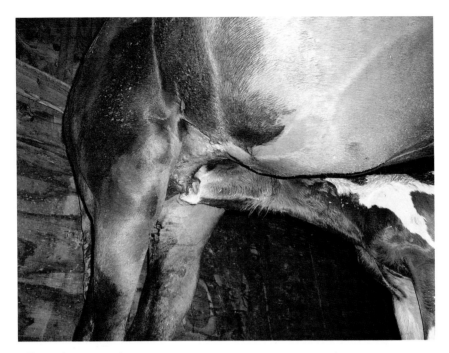

All together now—Awww!

behavior from the mare it is vital that you monitor the situation closely until you are certain that she will not injure or refuse to feed the foal.

Finally, perhaps forty-five minutes after birth, our new arrival made it to his feet and was able to stay there. Now his next challenge was to find the milk bar. This can also take a bit of time, and quite a few false starts. It's believed that foals are attracted to shadows at this time (which makes sense as the udder is under the mare and therefore in shadow) but they're not too picky about which shadows. Some people will recommend that you clean the udder after the foal is delivered and before they make their way onto their feet, to minimize the chances of the foal ingesting dirt/bacteria. Unless your mare got extremely dirty during the birthing process (in a normal foaling the mare will not bleed, so the only fluid present would be the allantoic and amniotic fluids), my feeling is that nobody cleans a wild mare's udder before baby first suckles and they do just fine, so why should a domesticated horse need to be cleaned? And, who knows, perhaps the fact that the foal has spent more than 300 days bathed in amniotic fluid means that having some of that present in the area of the udder will be a familiar scent (though I'm sure they can't smell it when they're inside the mare). I chose not to wash Moyie's udder, and after not too long a time (not as long as it seemed at the time) he finally found the udder and, after another few attempts, latched on to one of Moyie's teats for that all-important first drink. While he drank, Moyie would nuzzle and lick at his butt, I guess encouraging him, and she was happy to let me come in for a closer look, just to make sure he was actually drinking and swallowing. Everything was good, so I backed off again and just watched them getting to know each other. While they were occupied, I spread out a few bags of fresh shavings on the floor, just to make it nice and dry again. There is always some debate on which bedding is best for foaling time. One school of thought is that straw is best, because it doesn't stick to the wet foal so much as shavings would. Another school of thought is that shavings are better because they don't tangle the foal's legs like long pieces of straw might. My vet's opinion was that the best bedding was grass because it was most natural for the mare to foal out in the field. I wasn't going to leave her out because I wanted to be able to monitor things closely, so field wasn't an option, plus I know Moyie would have eaten her way through the bed if I gave her straw, so I stuck with her normal bedding of shavings. Even if you usually buy loose or cheap shavings which can be a bit dusty, I recommend for foaling time that you buy some of the compressed type as they have had the dust extracted and so will be easier on little lungs just learning to breathe.

When Moyie delivered the placenta, I made sure to go back into the stall so I could pick it up as soon as it was delivered. This was almost the ickiest part of the whole process, as I took the placenta out of the stall so that I could lay it out flat on the mats at the front of our barn. The common practice is to lay the entire thing out flat and make sure it's intact. This is an extremely important step, because any retained pieces of placenta can cause severe infection, even leading to post-foaling laminitis, and if a retained placenta situation is not dealt

with immediately it can be fatal to the mare. Moyie's was absolutely fine, so after taking a photograph of it to send to my vet, I folded up the placenta and put it into a garbage bag. Since we have a refrigerator in the barn, I actually put the bagged placenta into the fridge until I was able to take it to our dumpster. The side shown in the photo is the outside of the placenta; the inside is a deep red color.

Something else I found on the stall floor just after the foal was born called the hippomane is a soft, flat "thing" about six inches long. This contains high concentrations of salts such as calcium, magnesium, etc. and forms within the allantoic fluid that surrounds the amnion, the bag in which the foal spends its pre-birth life. It's a bit unusual to find it, so I thought a photograph might be helpful

for reference. In the old days, at least in Scotland, I had heard it called the "milt," and there are a lot of old wives' tales about it. One is that it actually comes out of the foal's mouth at birth, that it forms in there during the pregnancy to prevent fluid from entering the foal's lungs. Another tale says that it helps to shape the foal's tongue. Some people will tell you that it's good luck (well, I suppose it is, in the same way as a four-leaf clover is good luck—you're *lucky* if you find it!). Some would even tell you that it should be thrown up onto the roof over the stall, to protect the newborn foal. There is also folklore which says that the hippomane, when dried and ground into powder, is a powerful aphrodisiac.

The other milestone to watch for is that the foal passes the meconium successfully. The meconium is the small amount of poop which has accumulated in the foal prior to birth, and if this isn't passed it can cause problems. Some people even give a newborn foal an enema to help this along. The meconium is usually quite hard and dark in color, looking more like big rabbit or deer poop than anything a horse normally produces. Our boy passed his meconium "by the book," so maybe Moyie had been reading it to him during her pregnancy!

I stayed in the barn a few more hours and spent most of the time looking over the wall into Moyie's stall. I had by now emailed my vet some photos of the foal and also the one of the placenta, along with a quick rundown of the important points of how long it had taken for the foal to stand/suckle/pass meconium. He replied within the hour, and seemed as pleased as we were by how everything had gone. Pretty quick, pretty easy, and very textbook. But there are some important basic details and milestones to be aware of, so let's run through them here.

Newborn Normals

The fact sheet pictured here outlines the most vital information regarding your newborn foal, including normal vital signs. Contact your vet for advice/assistance if you notice anything outside of these parameters.

An easy-to-remember guideline for "what should happen when," is simply 1, 2, 3.

- One hour maximum for the foal to get to its feet.
- Two hours maximum for the foal to successfully nurse from the mare.
- Three hours maximum for the mare to pass the placenta.

The Newborn Foal Fact Sheet
Amanda M. House, DVM, DACVIM
University of Florida CVM

Normal Behavior:
    Suckle reflex: within 5 minutes of birth
    Sitting sternal within 10 minutes
    Standing up within 1-2 hours
    Nursing within 2-3 hours
    Pass meconium in 6-8 hours or sooner

Physical Examination:
    Temperature: 99-102 F
    Heart rate: 80-120 beats/minute
    Respiratory Rate: 20-40 breaths/minute
    Gums: pink and moist, capillary refill time < 2 seconds
    Pass pasty feces 3-5 times per day (but often hard to see in stall)

Remember to:
    Check IgG in all foals – stall side blood test
    Have vet check ALL foals at 12-24 hours old (the sooner the better)
    Normal IgG = 800 mg/dl or higher
    Dip umbilical stump with dilute Nolvasan 2-3 times in the first day of life

Time to Intervene:
    Retained placenta in mare > 3 hours
    Weak or unable to stand
    Has not nursed within 3-4 hours
    No colostrum or milk from dam
    No meconium passed, bloated or colicky
    Hypothermia (Temp < 99) or fever
    Diarrhea
    Difficulty breathing
    Not nursing well, lethargic, heart or respiratory rates too fast
    Lameness or swollen joint

Please remember to call your veterinarian if you have any concerns. We are available at the University of Florida 24 hours a day at 352-392-2229.

Reproduced by kind permission of Dr. Amanda House, DVM, DACVIM, University of Florida CVM.

You should also have your vet, within the first twelve to twenty-four hours, carry out a blood test known as an IgG (immunoglobulin G) test, sometimes called a failure of passive transfer test. This test will let you know if the foal has received sufficient antibodies from the mare via the colostrum. If the foal's antibody levels are low, the vet can administer IV plasma to boost the foal's immunity. Low antibody levels, if left untreated, may lead to illness ranging from diarrhea to septicemia to joint ill (septic arthritis).

Potential Problems

Let's assume that you've gone through the first stage part of labor, and your mare is now absolutely, definitely having her foal. Problems at foaling *do* require professional intervention unless you want to risk losing mare or foal or both. This is absolutely not the time to worry about being hit with a vet bill (even if it turns out to have been unnecessary). If you see any of these signs or symptoms, *call the vet*!

- Her water breaks but there is no further progress even though the mare is straining: It may be helpful to walk the mare to try to help her reposition the foal so that foaling may continue naturally, but call the vet *first*!
- The mare is rolling or thrashing excessively: Obviously she will roll and reposition herself during labor, but you know your mare best and if it seems as though she is panicked, she probably is, because she knows that something isn't as it should be.
- The amniotic fluid is stained brown or green: This means that the foal passed some of the meconium prior to birth. This indicates that the foal was stressed during the birth process. Problems can result from this, including swelling of the brain, which leads to Neonatal Maladjustment Syndrome (NMS) which covers a variety of less scientifically named conditions such as barker, wanderer, dummy foal, or convulsive syndrome. With NMS, the foal may initially appear normal but then within the first twenty-four hours suffer complete loss of suck reflex, convulsions, inability to stand, etc. The good news is that NMS-affected foals, given time and correct care, may often make a full recovery, though it can take up to thirty days for the foal to return to a normal state.
- Red bag: This is a colloquial term for a situation in which the placenta has begun to separate from the uterus prematurely. Instead of seeing the shiny, smooth white bag of the amnion begin to protrude from the vulval lips, a

dark red bag is seen instead. This is the allanto-chorionic membrane (which in a normal foaling will have ruptured to allow the allantoic fluid to escape, what we know as the water breaking). In this occurrence, the placental separation means that the foal is no longer receiving oxygen from the mare as it should, and this stimulates breathing to commence. Clearly, since the foal is still contained within the amnion, bathed in the amniotic fluid, this presents a severe risk of drowning. In this situation the allanto-chorionic membrane must be opened immediately, and the amnion will also need to be cut open, and you must assist the mare in delivering the foal as quickly as possible. Unless your vet lives next door, you will need to take action yourself because the vet will not arrive in time to save the foal.

- Malpresentation: The foal should be delivered in what is sometimes called the diver's stance, with both forefeet leading, facing down, and the muzzle lying on top. One forefoot will be a bit ahead of the other to assist the shoulders in passing through the pelvic hoop. There are a few malpresentations which may occur: breech, where the foal is presented butt-first; backward, where the hind legs are coming first; inverted, where the foal has failed to flip over; head bent back; one leg back, etc. If you don't have two forefeet and a muzzle, it's time to call the vet.

- Foal not breathing: Obviously this will need to be dealt with immediately, but you should still call the vet to check for any problems which may have been caused by hypoxia (lack of oxygen). It isn't unusual for the foal to be delivered with no sign of breathing, but the foal will often gasp as the chest is being delivered, and this expands the lungs and stimulates a normal breathing rhythm. Normal breathing will generally be established within thirty seconds of the foal's hips passing out of the birth canal. If the foal does not begin to breathe normally within thirty to sixty seconds, you must begin resuscitation immediately. Horses are not able to breathe through their mouths, so resuscitation is carried out in the following manner:

- Extend the foal's head to open the airway and ensure that the nostrils are clear of amnion and mucus/fluid.
- Kneeling between the foal's head and forelegs, place your hand farthest from the foal beneath the muzzle, holding the lower nostril closed.
- Place your mouth over the upper nostril and breathe into the nostril enough to raise the chest only a small amount.
- Release both nostrils to allow carbon dioxide to be exhaled, then repeat. You should maintain this rhythm at around twenty-five breaths per minute until the foal begins to breathe spontaneously.
- When the foal is breathing independently, it is helpful to move them from a prone position so that they are propped up on their chest as this makes breathing a bit easier.

- Stillbirth. Sadly, despite best efforts, foals are sometimes born dead, often due to the umbilical cord having been obstructed or compressed during birth. If the foal is not able to be successfully resuscitated, it is recommended that you leave the mare with the foal for a time, to allow her to satisfy herself that the foal is dead. Once she has become convinced of this, she will show no further interest in the foal, and at this time you can remove the foal without causing the mare undue distress. If the foal's body is removed before the mare has accepted the death then she may become frantic looking for her foal, so allow her the time to understand. If you are unfortunate enough to lose your foal, you should be watchful that your mare does not develop mastitis due to the milk in her udder not being used. Your vet can advise on the best way to "dry up" the mare or stop milk production. Alternatively, your vet or others may know of a foal who has been orphaned by the death of a mare, and it may be possible to offer your mare as a nurse mare. This of course is a prolonged commitment as your mare will be needed for many months until the orphan has been weaned.

- Mare hemorrhages. Mares do not generally bleed significantly during foaling, but on rare occasions a branch of the artery supplying the uterus may hemorrhage either at time of foaling or some hours after (this is why a twitch must not be used for the first few days post foaling, as the elevation in blood pressure it causes could precipitate hemorrhage). This causes a great deal of pain, usually evidenced by the mare displaying colic-like symptoms of abdominal discomfort, sweating, pawing, and anxiety. The mucus membranes will also be pale due to blood loss. The hemorrhage may be naturally contained and controlled by the pressure of the broad ligament, in which case the prognosis is usually good, although it may take several weeks for full recovery, with the mare suffering anemia and jaundice. If the hemorrhage breaks through into the peritoneal cavity, the mare will bleed to death and, sadly, there is little that can be done due to how quickly this will occur.

- Death of mare. On occasion, the mare may die due to complications of birth (hemorrhage, etc.), leaving you with an orphaned foal. If the mare has been able to give the foal its first feeding then sufficient colostrum may have been ingested to provide the necessary antibodies, but if not then colostrum must be acquired and given to the foal. You will have to either find a nurse mare for your foal (your vet can probably help with this as they will doubtless have other clients with mares foaling) or you will have to feed the foal yourself. This is quite an involved subject, so I think it merits a little section of its own.

Feeding the Orphan Foal

Feeding a foal yourself is a very labor intensive process, as the newborn foal will need to be fed at least every hour for the first week or so and then only a little less frequently over the following few weeks. Commercial foal milk replacers are available from feed stores, although some people do make their own, but this is definitely something about which you must consult your vet. (For convenience, I will refer to what the foal is being fed as "formula.")

The orphaned foal will need to be fed using a bottle. You can use a baby bottle fitted with a larger nipple such as those manufactured for feeding lambs, though for the first few days a human type nipple with the hole enlarged slightly will suffice. Of course, foals will quickly graduate to needing larger amounts of formula which may not fit in a baby bottle meant for humans. Fortunately, you can purchase bottles intended for feeding foals, or I have known people to use a clean soda bottle fitted with an appropriate nipple. The alternative is to introduce the foal to bucket feeding. This may be done immediately or after a few days of bottle feeding, but the principle remains the same. You should use a wide plastic bucket, preferably brightly colored so the foal may easily find it. Pour the formula into the bucket, then dip your finger into the formula and slip your finger into the foal's mouth (don't worry, they have no teeth yet!), letting him suck and get the taste of the formula. If the foal doesn't suck voluntarily, moving your finger against the upper palate and tongue should stimulate the nursing response. Slowly move the foal to the formula, so that he is drinking from the bucket, then gently remove your finger. Some foals learn more quickly than others, but if removing your finger causes him to stop drinking, simply wet your finger again and try again. It may take a little time, but just be patient and the foal will figure it out.

Once your foal has accepted that his "mom" is a strange-looking plastic thing filled with milk, you can hang a bucket of formula in the stall at a convenient height/position. The formula must be replaced twice a day, with the bucket being thoroughly washed between fillings. Utilizing two buckets is even better, so you can hang a fresh bucket of formula while taking the other for washing. The foal may drink as often as they wish, which is clearly a more natural arrangement than bottle feeding (and, let's face it, it's far less labor intensive for you!).

The foal will work up to consuming four to five gallons of formula per day. This is about how much a mare produces per day at peak lactation, and research suggests that there is little danger of the foal overeating. In addition to the milk, you must also provide your foal with water to drink, ensuring that this is also kept clean and fresh (even if the foal isn't yet showing interest).

An orphan foal who is being fed milk replacer will generally be switched to solid food sooner than a foal being raised naturally by a mare. Provided that this is done judiciously and with veterinary input, this should cause no problems with development. The usual practice is to begin offering a small handful of milk replacer pellets when the foal is around a week old. It may be helpful to place a few pellets directly into the foal's mouth, since he has no mother showing him how this eating thing works. The amount can be increased until the foal is eating two or three pounds of pellets, and at this time he can also be offered a small amount of "creep" feed. There are feeds specifically formulated for nursing foals, or you may already be using a feed which is suited to all age groups. Either way, follow the instructions on the feed bag, because overfeeding a foal with grain may certainly cause problems. The foal can also be given small amounts of good quality hay, or turned out to pasture, from a few weeks of age. Once your foal is eating four to six pounds of milk pellets and/or creep feed per day, you can start to wean him off the liquid formula. This may be possible as early as nine weeks of age, but you should definitely be guided by your vet's advice and recommendations in this regard.

In the natural course of things, a foal learns a great deal about just being a horse from its dam, but when there isn't a mare in the picture, it is very easy for a foal to lack basic socialization skills and manners. I once knew a beautiful young mare whose manners and understanding of human personal space were terribly bad. This mare had been orphaned and raised by, of all people, a horse trainer/instructor and they would interact with the foal as though they were also a horse, playing with the foal and allowing it to play with them. Now, maybe it's cute when a week old foal rears on its hindlegs and "waves" at you with its front hooves but, trust me, it's *not* cute when a 16hh three-year-old horse is doing it! It is imperative that an orphan foal be educated to behave with good manners and respect, even more so than any other foal. If at all possible, the foal should be turned out with a good influence (even stabled together if space permits) such as an older mare who has raised foals in the past, a patient gelding, or even a donkey. *Someone* who will teach and reinforce good horse manners!

Horses are herd animals and I firmly believe that they are at their happiest when they understand the pecking order. In all cases you must be at the top of that pecking order. I'm not saying in any way that you need to be mean to any horse, but I have seen countless horses who have shown very clearly that when their owner/handler is timid, they become more difficult. The horse is reacting to the handler's lack of confidence and interpreting this as fear, and the horse therefore reacts by lacking confidence itself. When handled by a more experienced person, that same horse will behave in a markedly different way, because they are comforted knowing that the handler is in charge and will keep them safe from danger.

Chapter 5

Four on the Floor

NOW that our foal had arrived and he and Moyie were both in wonderful health, we could breathe again! Some people advocate giving the mare a warm bran mash as her first feed after foaling because this is very easily digested and also has laxative properties, so will hopefully make it a little easier for the mare to poop when her lady parts are understandably somewhat painful. On the other hand, this would be a sudden change in feeding, which is something that should never be done when your mare's systems have already been so taxed. I have never really been an advocate of feeding bran mashes, though in the old days it was very common that all horses would be given a bran mash on Sunday evenings (a throwback to how hunting horses were cared for). Anyway, I certainly wasn't going to give Moyie a bran mash, but what I did do was make her breakfast extra sloppy. She was already getting soaked alfalfa cubes in there, so I just added extra water to get more fluid into her.

I also removed the wrapping from Moyie's tail. The wrapping, as expected, was pretty nasty, so it went straight into the garbage. The nice thing about removing tail wraps, though, is that you don't have to unwind them. Just grip the top and pull straight down and off it comes.

Now, I know all new mommies, even new mommies of fur babies, think their newborn is perfect and gorgeous, but even putting on my "professional" hat, I couldn't find fault with him. He was and still is well marked with strong borders between his colors.

I don't think I even mentioned yet what his color *is*, did I?

He is a bay tobiano, so his "base" color is bay (like Moyie) and his paint pattern is tobiano. A tobiano horse has white-haired patches on their coat with pink skin under the white hair. As I understand it, one of the characteristics which makes a horse tobiano as opposed to overo, sabino, etc. is that a tobiano horse has dark, sort of halo/shadow markings at the borders of their white patches. Check. Another is that the legs and feet are white. Check. (Though our boy has mixed feet, some solid and some striped.) Of course, the defining factor in this case was that I asked Amber, the ever-patient and helpful stallion owner, and she agreed with me that our colt was a bay tobiano.

Now, remember I mentioned the meconium? The rabbit-pellet first poop? Once that has passed, since the foal is now drinking milk, digestion is taking place and that means more poop. This poop isn't rabbit pellets, but it's not "normal" horse poop either. Like a human baby, your new foal is on an entirely liquid diet and, also like a human baby, that means we're talking more goop than poop right now. The best way I can describe what our foal was now producing is thick yellow mustard. Baby was now producing a satisfying amount of yellow goop-poop, which is another great sign because it means that the whole gut system is working properly. One thing you do need to watch out for is that the poop isn't sticking to the foal's butt and hind legs, as it is an irritant and can cause scalding of the skin, which is obviously going to be painful. Soft poop is normal, diarrhea is not, and the vet should be called if you are concerned because obviously, like any other animal (including humans!) prolonged diarrhea will cause dehydration.

In the first few days of a foal's new life (i.e. outside of the mare) they should be closely monitored as their bodies are going through some serious changes. Prior to birth they have been in a temperature-controlled environment and haven't done much in the way of moving around. Or even breathing. Now they are breathing on their own, moving around (and having to deal with the pull of gravity), and having to regulate their own body temperature. Their eyes and ears are also having to learn to do their jobs at this time. If you are in a cold climate, depending on the time of year your foal is born (since many people do try to have their foals born as close to January 1st as possible), it's entirely possible that your new baby will need to wear a blanket at night until their system gets the hang of things. If a foal is born prematurely, this is an even bigger concern. I have known of very small foals who were just too little for even a foal blanket, who ended up in a very fetching outfit of an old sweater covering their body and forelegs. Cute and effective.

As well as watching over baby, you also need to keep a close eye on your mare after she's given birth. Mares can obviously have post-foaling problems (thankfully Moyie had none at all) and if these are overlooked until they become serious issues, you face the risk of losing your mare and having to hand rear your foal (or try to find a nurse mare). Thankfully these problems are fairly rare, but you should be on the lookout for any bleeding (unlike humans, mares do not generally bleed after giving birth, due to the fact that their placenta attaches to the uterus differently) or uterine prolapse, where the mare essentially delivers the entire uterus (I'm vastly oversimplifying, but you get the idea). This condition requires *immediate* veterinary attention. The final major issue to watch out for is post-foaling laminitis, as briefly mentioned above. This can be caused by retention of placenta, which is why you must check the placenta for completeness once it is delivered. Even small pieces of retained placenta will release toxins which can cause severe laminitis, so if you check the placenta and it is *not* complete, you must call the vet to come and assist the mare. The usual practice is to administer oxytocin to stimulate the mare to deliver the remaining piece/s (or the entire placenta if she has not passed this within three to four hours of delivering the foal). If there is prolonged retention, your vet may also give antimicrobial drugs to prevent problems occurring. Please also be aware that, in the event that you need to restrain your mare for any reason over the three days or so after foaling, you must *not* use a twitch as this increases blood pressure and could potentially cause hemorrhage.

In their first few days, the foal will eat, sleep, poop, and pee. It can obviously be harder to catch them peeing, since they don't exactly hang out an "occupied" sign, but if you do see the foal urinating, the urine should be clear, and the foal should not seem to be straining unduly to pass urine. The urine should also, obviously, be coming from the appropriate place only. Foals may sometimes be affected by a condition called patent urachus. Simply put, the urachus is a tube which allows waste products to be eliminated by the fetal foal via the mare. This tube should naturally seal itself when the foal is born, but occasionally it either doesn't seal or doesn't seal completely. This can lead to urine continuing to leak from the umbilicus (navel stump) which is clearly not good. The degree varies from an occasional drip and moist looking navel area to an actual stream of urine when the foal urinates, and if untreated may cause potentially severe infection. It is possible for patent urachus to close on its own, but in most cases treatment will be required, including antibiotics to reduce the chance of infection spreading and application of a barrier cream to protect the skin around the navel. The tube is then closed either by chemical cautery (not really as awful as it sounds—a cauterizing agent such as iodine or silver nitrate is used) and this causes the tube to gradually close. If this still doesn't resolve the problem, surgical intervention is required. Regardless of the treatment ultimately required, if your foal has urine coming from someplace it shouldn't, the vet must be informed immediately.

Hubby came back out to the barn a bit after I'd fed, and we admired our new colt yet again, then decided he needed a name. At this time, sadly, my husband's stepfather was terminally ill (he in fact passed away only a few weeks after our foal was born). His name was George, and so in his honor we gave our colt the barn name of Geo. After a little consideration, we had decided to keep Moyie and Geo in the stall for this first day, just to give them some more time to bond properly, and also because Moyie was an older mare and we wanted to allow her a bit more time to recover. Moyie ate everything she was given, and her feed had now increased even more, as a lactating mare requires additional nutrition to allow her to produce the milk required for a hungry baby. Also make sure

Geo: as you can see, he was very excited to have a name!

that her water is kept topped up, as obviously milk production requires fluids, too!

While the mare knows the foal by smell (partly because she has cleaned his coat of amniotic fluid so learned him intimately) the foal is actually less clear on exactly who she is at the moment. Right now she's just that big thing the food comes from, and while the foal will follow her shape, he isn't yet tuned in to her scent. This is why it's advisable, if you have more than one mare foaling, that you keep them separated for a few days, to ensure each mare has imprinted on their foal. There was actually a fairly well documented case years ago where two Thoroughbreds were found, by blood typing, to have been accidentally switched shortly after birth. What happened was that the mares were turned out together quite soon after both had foaled and the foals, having not fully imprinted with their dams, switched. This meant that each foal's pedigree had been incorrectly registered, so it was basically a paperwork issue, but still quite interesting. We didn't have this potential problem to contend with since we only had one foaling mare, but it's still a good idea to allow the mare and foal plenty of alone time.

There is some controversy around "imprinting" the newborn foal. Some people advocate strongly that the foal should be handled quite thoroughly by the human handler, with much rubbing of the body and handling of the ears, head, legs, etc. This is thought to produce a horse which will be more easily trained in the future. There was a lot of publicity around this theory/practice many years ago, and it became quite popular. But like so many things with horses, it fell out of favor, probably at least in part because it became rather watered down as it was done by more and more people with less and less experience or understanding of what the initial proponent intended. The other side of the coin would be people who rather religiously avoid contact with the mare and foal after birth, so long as both are well. I know of many breeders of Clydesdales whose only contact with the pregnant mares and resultant foals is to look at them across the field, until it comes time for weaning the foals. I met one handsome colt foal who had lived out on the hills until the day before a popular annual "show and sale" of Clydesdales, when his breeder literally went out on his ATV and lassoed the colt then brought him in to be bathed and groomed and taken to the sale. I guess that does speak to the wonderful nature of Clydesdales though, that he went from being basically a wild horse to being handled, hauled, and shown in one day! One Clydesdale breeder friend goes the opposite way, constantly being in the foal's space, which I know by experience has resulted in horses who do *not* understand the concept of personal space. Sounds cute, but when a 17.3hh three year old is trying to sit in your lap, it gets less cute very quickly.

I don't believe in imprint training the foal, at least not in the intrusive way that many do (or at least did when the practice was most in favor), but I do believe that the foal needs to be accustomed to human presence and minor interference. Always bear in mind, of course, your mare's feelings on the matter. If your mare is having her first foal, she may be rather foal proud and not welcome your attention to her new baby, so just make sure that whatever you choose to do, you do it safely.

If you think the foal is not nursing (you can check the mare's udder, if it is still swollen tight with milk, the foal is not feeding properly), you need to monitor them to make sure the mare is allowing the foal to suckle, as some mares are ticklish or may find it painful. If the mare is not allowing the foal to suckle, you may need to hold the mare on her halter to allow nursing. If the problem is that the foal is not trying to suckle, you may want to call the vet.

Chapter 6

Room to Roam

IT is very important for the foal's development (as well as the mare) that they have ample turnout time in a safe area. You want an area which is large enough for the mare and foal to exercise, but not so big that the mare may take off galloping, because the foal *will* try to keep up with her. In the wild they will do this if they are trying to escape from a predator, but otherwise wild horses don't tend to spend all their time running around. Unfortunately, one of the things we have done by domesticating horses is to change their behavior so that they often *do* take off running when they're turned loose, especially if they have been confined more than they are accustomed to. So, you want to make sure that you have a safe area but not an entire large field.

Our front field is around five to six acres, much too large to allow them free rein, so we sunk fence posts around a small section of the front field so we could easily move Moyie and Geo from stall to field and back again. We used orange mesh fencing, the plastic stuff you will often see at construction sites. This is secure enough to keep them in unless they *really* want out, brightly colored so that they see it easily, and four feet high. As this was always intended to be a short-term restricted area, there was no point in spending a lot of money on more substantial fencing (and the posts would later be removed and used elsewhere).

Now, I was fairly confident that Moyie wouldn't go crazy when she was turned loose, as she's a pretty sensible mare most of the time and had only been in her stall for one day. But just in case, what often helps is to put them out without feeding them first, so their first priority will be to eat, not run. I gave Moyie a little hay, but held back her grain feed to give to her in the field. The other horses were put out in the back field, where they could catch a glimpse of Geo but not make contact with him at all, then it was time for some freedom.

One quick note here about first turnout (and I'm sure my editor hates me for my sudden, random thoughts that I stick in, but that's how my brain works). In general, I would say the sooner you can let your mare and foal have a bit of freedom, the better, but there are obviously some things you must first consider. Assuming you have had your vet check the foal on day one, they may recommend the foal be confined a bit longer, perhaps due to the legs being weak or crooked, to allow for things to improve before the joints and bones are put under the stresses of running around. Alternatively, if you are in a cold climate, weather may not be conducive to a new foal being outdoors (people who are fortunate enough to have an indoor arena or even a large, safe barn space may use these for an indoor version of turnout).

Since Geo's legs were good and it was Florida in May, we had no worries about weather, so I put on Geo's cute little foal slip and got Moyie's halter on, too. As a general rule, the most experienced person (in this case, me) should deal with the foal, but my husband decided he would take Geo while I took Moyie. The foal will obviously follow their mother, but Geo's eyesight hadn't quite adjusted from the darker environment of the barn and he broke away from my husband, charging at full speed into the field fence instead of going through the gateway! He bounced off and fell on his furry little butt (Geo, not my husband), but was completely uninjured and also now a little bit more willing to be directed to follow Moyie.

Foals really can't be led right away. If they feel the pressure of someone pulling on their lead, they will lean against the pressure, not yield to it, as they haven't yet learned what we want. You can better direct them by cradling your arms around their bodies and directing them along. Some handlers used to carry the foal, but I think that practice has rather gone the way of the dodo bird. After all, Geo was almost 10hh at birth and probably weighed about 120 pounds (newborn foals are generally around 10 percent of their mother's weight). Now, 120 pounds isn't really *that* heavy, but 120 pounds of wriggling foal would be!

Once we got them into the field, I took off Moyie's lead rope but left her halter on in case I needed to catch her quickly. Geo also kept on his halter for the same reason. A correctly fitted foal slip isn't likely to get hung up on anything. Geo's wasn't as snug as I would have liked, because he had the tiniest little head when he was born (his muzzle fit easily into the palm of my hand) but it was safe enough. This is also a good reason to use a leather rather than nylon foal slip, because if the halter does get caught on something, leather will break more easily than nylon (nylon tends to stretch a lot before it will finally break).

I had brought Moyie's breakfast out to the fence line before we brought them out, so now I took the bucket into the field so she could eat while Geo explored his expanded world. She was such a good mommy that she kept getting pulled away from her feed when he would wander off, and she would start calling to him and chasing after him. Eventually, he decided that a snack was in order, so Moyie was able to return to her

One of the least blurry shots!

breakfast while he hit the milk bar. We watched them for a while. It's astonishing to see how fast a day-old foal can run, and you'll no doubt find, like me, that many of your photos these first few days are nothing but a blur of passing foal! It's like trying to take photos of flying hummingbirds. This first venture into the field was a good opportunity to get a better look at Geo's movement, as in the stall he had obviously had little room to move around. Everything looked good, and he had gained full control over those insanely long legs.

At this early stage you should be watching for anything that *doesn't* seem normal, perhaps a crooked leg or if the foal doesn't seem to be suckling regularly. Remember, if you're not sure, check the mare's udder, because at this time it should not be fat and full. The foal should be nursing regularly so that the udder is constantly being drained and refilling. The first four days or so after birth are the most critical, as this is when any major problems will become evident. Some conditions associated with neurological issues may not manifest immediately after birth, but the foal will seem to have normal behavior for the first few hours before being struck with convulsions or other symptoms. Many times a foal with these problems can be saved and hopefully with no lasting damage, provided that immediate action is taken. This is most definitely not a time to go with "Let's see if it gets better in a few hours!" Another issue you may notice, particularly in Thoroughbred foals, is that the pastern joints are very weak, often to the point of the fetlocks touching the ground. Normally this will resolve itself quite quickly (within the first day or so) but if it doesn't, you guessed it, call the vet!

Chapter 7

Foal Care

IF all is going well your mare is going to do the vast majority of foal care, and if everything seems to be progressing well then I firmly believe that she's best allowed to do it. Nature has been doing this for a very long time and has a pretty good handle on things. Of course, there are some things you should watch out for, and some things you can do to give your foal the best start in life, and also to start them on the right ~~foot~~ hoof.

First Day, First Vet Visit

The newborn foal's body is undergoing massive adjustments and changes in the first hours of life, making the transition from being in utero where everything is done for them in terms of their nutrition and waste being passed through the mare to being an independent creature who must now deal with the world and everything that brings. During the first twelve hours, the composition of the foal's blood actually changes, with the most important change (at least the one we need to worry about and can actually *do* something about!) being the increasing concentration of protein substances known as immunoglobulins, but more commonly referred to as antibodies. The foal does not possess these at birth, and these are the super-important component of the colostrum within the first milk. The antibodies contained within the colostrum are absorbed through the foal's stomach lining and provide what is called a passive immunity (passive because the foal has been "given" the immunity by the mare and has not developed it by itself). If the foal does not receive sufficient colostrum, and therefore antibodies, then this is called *failure of passive transfer* and will result in the foal having a reduced resistance to infection. The antibodies can only be absorbed through the stomach lining up to around twenty-four hours of age, and after this it doesn't matter if the foal is receiving colostrum because they are unable to derive any benefit from it.

It is strongly advisable that your vet pays a visit to the foal on their first day, mostly so that the important IgG test may be carried out. I have seen timescales for this test recommending it be performed anywhere from twelve to twenty-four hours to forty-eight hours after birth. My own feeling is that the sooner it is done the sooner you know if further action is required. In the event that the IgG test shows that antibody levels are low, your vet can provide intravenous transfusions of plasma to improve the foal's immunity. On this first visit, your vet may also want to carry out a CBC (complete blood count) test. Any abnormal levels in this test could suggest that the foal may require antibiotics for a few days. Allow your vet to guide you on whether or not this is needed.

So what else will the vet do? Well, they will do a general health check, making sure that your new foal's temperature, pulse, and respiration are within normal parameters. They will check that the mucus membranes are of a healthy color and that the capillary refill time is normal (less than two seconds). They will also check that the limbs are straight (though this can change very much over the foal's early years, which we'll touch on later), the eyes clear, and that the foal appears to have normal reactions to sound, etc. They will also make sure that the umbilical stump looks to be properly sealed and clean.

The vet will also check the mare at this time, and if you have kept the placenta because you're not sure whether it is intact, they can take a look and tell you. If it isn't intact, they can treat the mare accordingly. Your mare's general demeanor will be assessed, which is nothing more than the vet knowing your mare's normal temperament and judging whether she is showing anything very out of the ordinary, or at least anything which wouldn't be explained by the often exhausting process of foaling. Her vulva may be quickly examined for undue damage (and if she previously had a Caslicks operation, this may be reestablished at this time if deemed necessary). The udder will also be checked.

First Week, the Adaptive Period

The first vet visit should take place the foal's first day, but in the first four days or so (known as the adaptive period) you should be alert for any behavioral changes which may indicate problems, as these can take a little time to develop. If a foal is initially behaving normally and then they stop nursing or stop following the mare, or display anything else which is markedly different from their previous behavior, you must be very watchful and contact your vet if you are concerned. These problems may have neurological symptoms such as Neonatal Maladjustment Syndrome or may be more physical in nature such as joint ill or septicemia. Septicemia is a term covering a generalized infection (regardless of the causative bacteria/infection/virus) which is spread via the bloodstream to the majority of the organs and tissues, if not the entire body. In newborn foals the most likely scenario is that infection has entered via the navel stump (hence the need to treat this with diluted iodine or similar antiseptic treatment). This is a very serious problem and must be treated quickly.

Symptoms of septicemia include:

- Loss of appetite or inability to nurse due to diminished strength of the suck reflex.
- Foal not able to get to his feet/remain standing.
- Dehydration. This can be judged by taking a pinch of skin on the foal's neck. When released, the skin should almost immediately return to a flat position. If it remains pinched,

the foal is dehydrated. Another sign of dehydration is that the eyeballs will appear sunken in their sockets.

- Diarrhea.
- Temperature outside of normal parameters. It is not uncommon for a young animal's temperature to *decrease* in response to infection rather than increase as you would expect, due to the newborn's systems not yet responding appropriately to infection. Therefore, an abnormally low temperature is just as significant as a fever.
- Respiration outside of normal parameters, either rapid or very slow.
- Depression/coma-like state.

If you observe any of these symptoms, you must contact your vet. If your foal is diagnosed with septicemia, it will require antibiotics and possibly intravenous fluids. Septicemia can progress rapidly, and is one of the leading causes of early foal mortality, so prompt action is necessary.

Another infection which may occur in the newborn (actually possible in any horse, but more common in newborns) is joint ill, or more properly called Infective Arthritis. This condition may affect a single joint or all of the foal's joints, and is sometimes precipitated by septicemia. Symptoms of joint ill would be sudden, severe lameness along with warm, painful swelling of the affected joint/s. As with septicemia, the foal may lose their appetite and appear depressed, with temperature outside of normal parameters. Joint ill requires quick and quite aggressive treatment if permanent damage is not to be sustained. Treatment is carried out to kill the infectious microbes and minimize the joint damage caused by the bacteria and the white blood cells which are fighting the infection. This treatment will involve antibiotic drugs, possibly for several weeks, and the joint/s will be flushed with a large needle and sterile fluid to remove debris. This flushing must be done as soon as possible after joint ill is diagnosed, and may sometimes need to be repeated. Prognosis depends on how quickly the condition is diagnosed and treatment started, and how quickly the foal responds. The longer the infection is allowed to continue, the greater the chance of permanent damage to the cartilages of the joint and the development of secondary joint disease. A foal who is suffering from joint ill in many joints has a very guarded prognosis (I actually have a friend who lost a Clydesdale foal to joint ill), so veterinary assistance must be sought without delay.

Other conditions which may arise in the first days of the foal's life include meconium colic (which is why it is so important to pay attention that the foal successfully passes the meconium). Meconium colic is caused by the foal not passing the feces which have accumulated prior to birth, and is evidenced by the usual colic symptoms of pain, rolling, lying in awkward positions, and turning the head to look at the flanks. This can occur at repeated intervals for hours or even days. Treatment, as with any colic treatment, includes pain relieving drugs and administration of oil via a stomach tube. Many people choose, as a matter of routine, to give foals an enema shortly after birth to try to help things along.

Ruptured bladder is thankfully much less common but still a dangerous and severe condition. If the bladder is ruptured (perhaps due to damage during birth or an anatomical defect/improper fetal development), urine will escape through the bladder wall into the peritoneum. Symptoms will not usually develop until two to five days after foaling, since it takes a little time for enough urine to be produced and escape to actually show symptoms. Symptoms are quite similar to those of meconium colic, and the abdomen will also swell and continue to increase due to the accumulation of urine. If this is not treated, the pressure will eventually compress the lungs and basically suffocate the foal, so clearly wait-and-see is *not* a viable option! Diagnosis is confirmed via ultrasound and treatment requires surgery to drain the urine and repair the damage to the bladder. The good news is that if this condition is diagnosed and treated early, foals usually recover completely with no lasting effects.

One more potential major issue to be watchful for is any problems arising with the new foal's umbilical stump. In the vast majority of foals, the umbilical cord will break, seal, dry up, shrivel, and come away all by itself over the course or a week or two. But sometimes things don't go quite to nature's plan, so if the umbilical area seems unduly swollen or enlarged, you should have your vet take a look. Swelling may indicate an abscess, which will obviously require treatment, or it could be an umbilical hernia caused by the abdominal wall not closing as it should. A hernia in this case is a small piece of the foal's intestine which is protruding through the hole in the abdominal wall. These often resolve naturally, but should be examined as there is a danger of strangulation to the protruding intestine.

Outside of staying alert for any signs of these few major problems, in your foal's first week you should basically just be mindful of anything which seems "off." Likewise, keep an eye on the mare and how she is interacting with the foal. Particularly, if the foal seems to be trying repeatedly to nurse but acts as though the milk bar has run dry by trying both sides or butting at the udder in an attempt to get milk flowing, make sure to check that your mare still has milk. It isn't unknown for a mare to lose her milk, and clearly in this situation you will need veterinary intervention and, at least temporarily, an alternate source of nutrition for the foal. On the opposite end of the scale, if the udder remains swollen tight and full, you should monitor whether the foal is nursing. Sometimes a mare may find the process ticklish or even painful if her foal is a little too enthusiastic, and if she is refusing to let the foal suckle, you need to restrain the mare to allow the foal to feed. Fortunately, this will mostly happen around the first attempt at nursing, especially with a first-time mom, and once they understand what is happening they will settle. Of course, one other thing may make your mare suddenly a little resistant to her foal nursing. Teeth! Foals are born without teeth, but in the first week or so of life their upper and lower central incisors will come through in the center of the upper and lower jaw, two teeth on each. So, now your mare is dealing with four (admittedly small) teeth every time the foal nurses. Even the best tempered mom will occasionally give her offspring a nip on the butt or back leg as a warning about overenthusiastic use of these tiny weapons!

Don't be too alarmed if an otherwise perfectly healthy foal develops a case of diarrhea at around one week old. This is very common and caused by fluctuating hormone levels in the milk as the mare enters her first post-foaling estrus period. This is known as the foal heat, and in the wild a mare will very often be bred by the herd stallion on this heat cycle. Even in domesticated horses, some breeders will breed the mare on the foal heat to try to ensure an early foaling date the following year.

First Months

Now that you're through that ultra-critical first week, you can relax a little bit from being hyper-vigilant about, well, everything, and settle into the usual kind of "Did he have that bump yesterday?" worrying that you do about any other horse. Admit it, what self-care horse owner *doesn't* have a healthy (hey, I say it's healthy!) level of paranoia when it comes to their horse's wellbeing? As you wrap your head around their arrival after such a long wait, and the amazement that such a huge animal even *fit* inside your mare, you also become more accustomed to the foal's normals.

Some people advocate leaving the foal halter on all the time, especially if the mare and foal will be living out at pasture, but since I prefer to have my horses stabled at night, there was no reason for this. I also think that the more times the foal gets the halter put on and removed, the more accustomed to this process they will become. Another major reason to *not* just leave the halter on is that foals grow very quickly, and if you leave it on it may start to rub or cut into the face unless you are checking it regularly. Certainly if you are using a nylon foal halter, this really should not be left on during turnout as it will not break if the foal gets hung up on something.

At early stages, it isn't possible to lead your foal in the normal-horse way, since they don't understand what you're trying to do. Pulling on the halter will cause them to move back into the pressure, which is completely the opposite of what we want! Teaching them to lead takes a little work, and there are various tips and tricks to do this, but I found that just a bit of perseverance and some hand pressure on the hindquarters was sufficient to build the understanding of what the human wants. You can also use a soft lead rope around the hindquarters to help encourage forward movement, but whichever way you choose to do it, hand pressure or rope, just make sure that you are giving gentle encouragement rather than trying to force the foal to move. If you try to *pull* the foal along, they will resist and this pressure may also injure their neck. Pushing too hard from behind could simply cause the foal to "fold" until they sit down, but very often if the foal is simply walked alongside the mare, their instinct to follow her will make them understand (at least that was our experience). I also heartily recommend that, while leading *any* horse, you do not loop the rope *around* your hand but rather zig-zag it across your palm, since this way you are far less likely to get your hand caught in the rope if a horse does spook or bolt. I generally hold the rope maybe six inches from the clip, folding it across my palm again so there is a decent sized loop below my hand, then hold the loose end in my left hand. This way if a horse does try to pull free I have a foot or two of rope that will "give" and afford me the chance to regain control.

It is usually recommended that two people are involved at all times when leading the mare and foal around, one for each animal, but in everyday life we don't always have an extra pair of hands to help us (well, I usually don't). If you do have to work alone, the best thing is to lead the mare from her right side, using a rope as usual, and hold the foal's halter (if your foal halter doesn't have a short strap already attached, as mine did, you can attach a shortened lead rope to give you something to hold) as the foal walks alongside. In our case, when we reached the paddock I would take them ten or twenty feet from the gate before turning them loose, allowing me to get back to the gate and close it safely. Of course, most of the time I can easily lead my adult horses with just a rope around their necks, no halter, which meant I didn't have to worry about removing Moyie's halter in the pasture. Your own mare's level of behavior may differ, and always make sure that safety and control are your first priorities.

Patience and perseverance with firm but gentle and, most importantly, consistent handling are the keys to helping your foal learn what is expected of them. Before allowing a behavior "because it's cute," consider whether it would be so cute from an adult horse. Mares do not wait until their foal is older to instill discipline and manners, and neither should you! I can't stress enough how important this is. Think of that ill-mannered toddler you've seen at the mall. Would you like your horse to throw tantrums because they don't want to be controlled? I certainly wouldn't! From day one your foal must be given clear guidance as to what is and is not acceptable behavior. Trust me, they will be much happier knowing what the rules are. Sure, they'll push the boundaries every so often, but that's just part of their learning and growing. Your job is to maintain those same boundaries firmly but kindly and they will develop into well-adjusted horses.

Now obviously your mare will be heavily involved in helping the foal to grow into a mannerly youngster, and at least initially they will be separated from any other horses. In fact, we kept ours separated by a wide space to avoid any of the other horses getting too interested when there was just a fence between them, and when we did allow over-the-fence contact it was pretty closely supervised until everyone got used to it. Well, except the couple of times that Moyie and Geo escaped from their nursery paddock, but I'll get to that in a minute. If you do have other horses and, like me, you prefer to let them have as close to a normal herd atmosphere as possible, then the foal will need to be introduced to the group.

We kept ours separate for the first couple of months, partly because our Quarter Horse mare can be very cranky with new horses (or even horses she knows!) and also because we have a big Thoroughbred gelding here who can be very protective of "his" girl Moyie and we didn't want him interfering with the foal. We used tough plastic construction netting as a temporary fencing solution to make our nursery paddock. The problem with this is of course that it has a degree of flexibility to it and will stretch under pressure, say when a big old Thoroughbred mare decides the grass is greener on the other side! And that's what Moyie clearly did one day. I looked out into the main field and saw our lovely mare and foal happily grazing, then realized that they weren't *supposed* to be in the main field! I headed out with her halter and captured the escapees, bringing them back to the nursery where I couldn't at first figure out how they had escaped. It seems she had pushed the fencing up while stretching under it, and probably Geo first made his way under the space and then mommy followed. I returned them and hoped it wouldn't happen again (yeah, I know, it was a forlorn hope). After it happened another couple of times, we decided that it was pointless to try to keep them confined, so we allowed them to have access to the whole front field while the other horses were turned out in the back field. We closely supervised the first across-the-fence interactions in case of any aggression from the adult horses, but there thankfully was only curiosity and interest, so we were safe to allow the two groups to be turned out in the adjacent fields. We carried on in this way for some months, then after a minor hurricane had passed through, leading to flooding

First meeting with the big Thoroughbred gelding who would become his buddy (and I'll freely admit that this is not ideal fencing!) closely supervised by Moyie.

which kept the horses in their stalls for a day or two, they were turned out as normal. Of course, having been confined to his stall for a couple of days, Geo was filled with energy and racing around like . . . well, like a foal who had been confined for a couple of days! But this day, playing and running around as you would expect, he was racing toward the fence between the two fields when he clearly realized that he was going far too fast to either stop or turn on wet grass. So, being a colt given to swift decisions, he opted for door number three and *jumped* the fence between the fields. To be clear, this fence is four feet high, and he cleared it from a gallop without even thinking twice! Which of course landed him in the adjacent field with the other horses. Even though they had been across-the-fence friends, I was obviously worried how the others would react to this interloper in their field, so I headed out to let him back into the correct field. The other horses got to Geo before I did, but their intent seemed to be to check he was okay after his high jumping hijinks, and I just opened the gate between the fields and shooed him back where he belonged. But this inadvertent introduction did allay any worries about how he would be received when we integrated the herd again, and in fact we did so just a couple of days later.

I believe it is very important for a young horse's education that they interact with as many other horses as possible (obviously only horses whose attitude you are comfortable with) and this has certainly proved to be true in our case. Moyie had already instilled correct behavior into her son, and the other horses now reinforced her teaching. Barbie in particular can be quite a cranky, stay-away-from-me mare, and Geo showed healthy curiosity but also made it clear that he understood everything Moyie had taught him. Even today, as a three-year-old stallion, if his big Thoroughbred buddy shows irritation with him, he will instantly display submissive mouthing behavior, which I credit entirely to Moyie's early lessons.

Deworming

During pregnancy your mare should have been maintained on her regular deworming schedule, and the foal will also require to be started on a deworming protocol. This will usually be done around two months of age, and you must make sure that the dewormer used is suitable for young foals as a couple of the chemicals are definitely not foal safe. A friend's young Clydesdale foal became deathly sick from a dewormer which was not at the time labeled as unsafe for young horses. The foal did recover, but died as a three year old, possibly from related complications. The more traditional dewormer chemicals such as Fenbendazole, Pyrantel Pamoate, and Ivermectin are generally considered safe for use in foals but of course always read the label and other information, and if necessary consult your veterinarian for advice. Better safe than sorry!

So your foal should be given their first dewormer at around two months of age, and it is recommended that you deworm on a rotating schedule (i.e. if you start with Fenbendazole, use Pyrantel Pamoate next, then Ivermectin, then back to Fenbendazole) at one- to two-month intervals. I feel like every month is rather a lot, but please follow your vet's advice in this regard, as different areas may have different levels of parasite burden. Once your foal reaches one year old, they may be added to your regular deworming program and dewormed in line with the mare and any other horses you have.

Vaccinations

Another important part of the growing foal's health routine is vaccination against disease. This does not typically have to be started until close to weaning time, as the foal has received antibodies from the mare's colostrum which carry it through the first few months. Generally, the first round of vaccinations will be done when the foal is around five months old, and even if (like me) you usually administer your own vaccines, I do strongly recommend having your vet do at least the first round in case of any complications from the injection. In our case this was actually the first time our vet even met Geo in person, so perhaps it wasn't the best introduction to this new person since from Geo's point of view this tall human entered his house, groped him a bit (to check that both testicles had descended properly) and then stabbed him in the neck with a needle.

The vaccines required will vary by your location, but in our case we use a combination vaccine which covers West Nile Virus, Eastern and Western encephalomyelitis, rhinopneumonitis (EHV-1 and EHV-4), influenza, and tetanus. This gives a broad coverage without the need for multiple needles poking the horse, which is less painful for them and less stressful for me when I do my vaccinations. Rabies vaccination is given separately and, since rabies is 100 percent fatal once symptoms appear, it is definitely not one you want to skip.

One other vaccine which may be given is for strangles (streptococcus equi). There is some debate over just how effective the vaccine for this really is, and the most commonly used one is administered via an intranasal route, a little bit like how dogs are given the bordatella (kennel cough) vaccine. I don't give any of my horses strangles vaccine, for a few reasons. One, because the efficacy isn't as high as the other vaccines. Two, because my horses are generally not in contact with "strange" horses (even at shows I do not permit my horses to make contact with other horses or to drink from communal troughs, etc.). Third, I have dealt with strangles many (many, many!) years ago and know that with appropriate treatment it is messy and icky but can be treated.

Whichever vaccines are required in your area or recommended by your vet, the usual practice is that the first vaccination is given, followed by a booster one month later, and thereafter the foal will be vaccinated annually or on the same schedule as your adult horses if you are in a region where some vaccines, such as West Nile, are administered more frequently.

Farrier Care

Hoof care must be started early in your foal's life. Your farrier probably won't need to do very much in the first couple of months, but the foal should be introduced to the farrier at the earliest opportunity. Our farrier was scheduled to visit a month or so after Geo's birth, so he paid close attention to what this strange man was doing to his mommy! On this visit our farrier just picked up a couple of Geo's feet for practice

(practice for Geo, not the farrier!).

It is important to bear in mind that it is *not* your farrier's job to teach your foal to pick up their feet! Yes, all young horses (and some older horses) will have days where they are a bit reluctant to pick up their feet, but your foal should be accustomed to having his/her legs and feet handled from a pretty early age. Try to not make a big deal about it. I suggest that when you clean your mare's feet (which obviously you should be doing at least daily anyway) you then move to the foal and ask for each foot. Run your hand down the leg to the fetlock, then apply gentle pressure while saying "up" (or whichever word you generally use to your horses—I know some people say "foot" instead). Don't try to *pull* the foot off the ground, but rather use just a bit of pressure to encourage the foal to lift it themselves. When they do pick up the foot, cup the hoof in your palm (try not to get too distracted by the cuteness) and just flick the brush of the hoof pick over the sole. You're not trying to actually clean out the hoof, just get the foal accustomed to the process. If you take the time each day to work with the foal on this, they will very quickly get the idea and not see it as anything other than part of their regular daily routine (which is kind of the point!). When it comes time for the farrier to do it, if the foal is less keen to pick up the feet for a stranger, I did find in our case that it helped initially if I first picked up the foot, then let the farrier take it from me. It was less stressful on Geo (and us) and he quickly understood that it didn't matter who asked for the foot. It was to be given. Sure, there were times where he would pull the foot away from me or the farrier, but it is important if this happens that you do not get angry with the foal. Instead, give a quick vocal reprimand (i.e. "no!" or "bad!") then ask for the foot again and praise when it's given. Someone I knew years ago called it the triple R of training horses: Reward, Reprimand, and Repetition. But the key with anything is, of course, consistency. You cannot expect the foal to learn something if you are not being consistent in what you are asking or accepting as good behavior.

By starting your foal's hoof care early, this allows your farrier to catch any problems before they develop into a major issue. In our case, when Geo was about four months old I noticed the day before our farrier was due that his right front foot looked very odd. He was standing on his tiptoe rather than the flat of his foot. This literally developed overnight. My farrier immediately recognized it as hyperflexion/contracted tendons and recommended I have my vet visit to assess the problem as soon as possible.

So what was actually wrong? Well, to put it very simply, hyperflexion or contracted tendons describes what happens when the long bones of the leg (cannon bone, etc.) are growing faster than the tendons can keep up. If your foal, who previously had perfectly normal looking feet and legs, is suddenly up on tiptoe on one (or more) legs, this is clearly not normal and must be addressed as soon as possible. The sooner the problem is identified and treatment started, the better the prognosis.

So, what is the treatment? Well, my vet visited a day or two later to assess the problem. He agreed with my farrier's opinion and approved of what had already been done. The farrier had trimmed the heels of that foot as much as he could, to encourage a more correct position. If an affected foal walks on their tiptoe, the heels will be worn down much less than the toes, allowing the heels to grow faster. This leads to the foal developing a very upright, boxy "club foot" which will exacerbate the problem. If this condition is not dealt with early (or if it is very severe), it is possible that the only possible solution will be surgery to cut the ligament and "free up" the tendon, but in our case, my vet's recommended treatment was just to keep the heels as short as possible and see if nature would take care of it. Fortunately I have a farrier rasp and am pretty comfortable using it so for the next few months, every week or two I would rasp down Geo's heels on that foot, with my farrier undertaking slightly more aggressive trimming on his visits. Within just a few months Geo's foot had returned to normal (though even now I am very watchful of the conformation of that foot!). We got

You can see how much more upright the right hoof/pastern is than the left.

lucky, really. Something which *could* have been a major issue was dealt with fairly painlessly and at the cost of only one vet visit.

Feeding of Mare & Foal

In the early months of your foal's life, your mare will be providing much of the nutrition via her 24–7 milk bar, but at a fairly young age the foal will begin trying out other things to eat. They will imitate their mother in grazing and eating hay (or trying to) and will very soon take an interest in whatever delights may be found in Mom's feed bucket. Some mares are willing to share (Moyie not so much) but you must consider what the mare is being fed and if it is suitable for a young foal.

Before we start on feeding of the foal, though, let's look at the mare. While the mare's nutritional requirements increased during pregnancy, particularly in the last trimester, lactation or milk production increases those even further. In fact, the feed that I use recommends a mare of Moyie's size in her third trimester should be getting between five and seven-and-a-half pounds of grain per day, but once the foal is born and she is producing milk this *doubles* to ten to fifteen pounds per day. Obviously, these amounts are for just the grain portion of the ration, not including hay/grazing, etc. but you can see that it's still a very substantial increase. Producing the milk needed for a hungry, growing foal takes a huge amount out of the mare, and you must make sure she is being fed appropriately so that she is able to maintain her own condition while feeding the foal. Though most mares will lose a little weight during this period, you don't want her becoming underweight because she's giving everything to the foal.

Some people choose to feed the foal a specifically made starter or "creep" feed designed for foals unless the feed already used is designed for all life stages and contains the necessary vitamins, minerals, etc. for a growing foal. There are special foal feeders available which are simply small square feeders with a metal grille on the top to prevent the mare's much bigger muzzle from getting in there and stealing the foal's food. This is more necessary if they are being fed different things, of course, but that was what I used for Geo's meals. I also tied Moyie loosely by her feed bucket and held Geo on a rope by his, just to enforce the idea of eating from your own "plate" and not helping others. I started Geo out with just a tiny handful of grain, a couple dozen pellets, and he's certainly his mother's son as he vacuumed it up pretty quickly! Some people say to wait until the foal is about a month old before offering feed, but I feel that it's best to listen to the foal. If you see they are trying to share with their mother, it's probably time to offer them their own little ration. After all, since the mare is still providing the vast majority of the nutrition via her milk, she's the one who really needs the food!

As the foal's appetite increases, you can increase the amount of grain they are receiving, but overfeeding is *not* recommended, partly because the foal's little stomach can only handle so much at a time, but mostly because overfeeding has been linked to Developmental Orthopedic Disease (DOD), also known as epiphysitis or physitis and/or Osteochondrosis (OCD). These conditions refer to abnormal activity in the growth plate (physis), most commonly the lower growth plate of the radius bone just above the knee, and is generally caused by too-rapid growth of the young horse. Some breeds are "encouraged" to grow quickly in their early years, particularly Thoroughbreds which are destined for the race track, so they are fed very high amounts at a young age. Some people also overfeed youngsters who are headed to the show ring, because of the myth that "fat" equals "healthy." With Geo, his ribs have always shown just a touch, and my vet has always commented that his weight is just right and told me *not* to get him fatter. In my opinion, overfeeding a young horse just to get it into work faster or to get a better placing at a show regardless of the long-term consequences is irresponsible and just wrong.

If you find that your foal is eating their own ration and helping themselves from their mother's bucket too, you should restrain the foal while the mare eats. If the foal wants to nurse, that's fine, but keep a rope on their halter so that you can prevent them from eating from the mare's bucket. Partly because the mare needs it more, and also if you are feeding the mare something with a high calcium content such as alfalfa or sugar beet pulp (both of which Moyie gets in her feeds), the excess calcium may contribute to the possibility of the foal developing DOD/OCD. There has been a lot of research into these conditions, and there are many possible causes, but mineral imbalance is certainly one of the possible causative factors, so avoiding excessive levels of anything seems a sensible approach. A simple rule of thumb is that the foal should not receive more than one pound of feed (per day) for every month of age. So, a three-month-old foal should not receive any more than three pounds of grain per day, split into two or three feedings. Please note that the yellow-mustard poop you became accustomed to on the foal's all-liquid diet will change once they start eating more solid food. The poop will look more like that of a large dog, but not "normal" horse poop yet due to the high liquid content of the diet.

Foal Education

During these first months, there are many things you can teach the young foal to make both your lives a bit easier later. Now, if your mare is good at things like standing quietly while tied or loading into a trailer, she will be a great ally/teaching tool, since her foal will be more inclined to follow her lead on things. Also, just having their dam around when trying new things will help keep the foal relaxed.

I also believe in treating any new experience for any horse in a rather pragmatic manner. Treating it less like, "This is new and you might find it scary but we're going to do it really slowly and carefully and it'll be okay," and more along the lines of, "This is happening and you'll be just fine." If your horse trusts you, they will follow your lead on things. This is why, within reason, I believe in doing "silly" things with horses. You always want to keep things safe, but I did things like putting empty shavings bags on Geo from a pretty young age, first on his back then on his head. And if/when it fell off, he was allowed to investigate it. I think that the more things you do which maybe aren't textbook, such as letting blanket straps fall and hit their legs or dragging the blanket off rather than carefully folding and lifting it, will help make the foal (or any horse) accept what is happening. It also means that if something does ever go wrong, they are more likely to behave calmly, since their mindset isn't going to be "this is going to kill me" but rather "okay, what's mom doing to me now?"

A natural extension of teaching the foal to lead is teaching the foal to stand tied. Bearing in mind that a horse's first line of defense, and their first reaction to threat, is to run away (the "flight" part of fight or flight), standing quietly while tied up is obviously an unnatural thing for them. The old school of thought (and I'm sure still practiced by many people) was that a fairly young foal should be tied directly to a solid object such as a wall/tree/post, using a strong halter and rope, and allowed to "fight it out" until they understood that being tied meant you stayed right where you were. This was done early on with young foals because they lacked the strength and weight to break free or hurt themselves in fighting the restraint. This practice has fallen out of favor, with many people talking of "learned helplessness" in which the foal, having accepted being tied and that they cannot escape, has "switched off" or given up trying as a result. This may produce the desired effect of the horse staying tied, but at the expense of the horse's mental wellbeing.

My approach to tying Geo wasn't to tie him to a wall or tree and let him fight. Initially, I would simply hold him onto his rope and not allow him to walk off. Then, I progressed to looping his rope around one of the thick posts which hold up the barn while I held the other end, so that if he did get panicky, I could release a bit of pressure so he didn't feel so trapped. It also helps if your mare ties well and you can tie her up at the same time so the foal can observe her reaction. I then would wrap the rope twice around the post to provide some friction and go about whatever I was doing in the stall. If Geo simply tried to move a little bit, the rope prevented it, but if he pulled back hard, it would slip. I would then tie his rope to the post and leave the stall for a few minutes, always keeping watch on his behavior so I could return if he started to panic. I'll admit that I don't often tie him up, simply because if I put his halter on and throw the rope over the front wall of his stall, he understands that he should stay there (this is what I do with most of my horses). It seems that he understands even light rope pressure means stay where you are. Of course, when we take him out to a show, I don't tie him to the outside of the horse trailer, simply because show grounds tend to be on fairly busy roads with wide open gates. Having seen at least one loose horse at a show, I don't want mine to be one of them!

The important thing to remember when teaching a young horse to tie up is take it slow and steady. You want to make it a pleasant experience for the horse, because it will make them accept it much quicker *and* make them not see it as a bad thing. Use a strong, well-fitting halter and a strong rope, and make sure the rope clip is also in good condition because these will often break before the rope or halter does. Always make sure that when you tie *any* horse, you are using a quick release knot, and make sure that the rope is tied high enough and short enough that the foal cannot get a leg over the rope. You don't need to create easily avoidable problems by being lax in the details.

Another thing the foal should learn at an early age is loading into a trailer. This is only practical if you have your own trailer or access to one where the mare and foal are living. Again, this should be done slowly and carefully, and often the best/easiest way to do it is simply lead the mare into the trailer, perhaps feeding her in there, and let the foal figure it out and join her. You can encourage the foal, perhaps with a gentle pat or pressure on their butt if they seem confused about stepping up into the trailer (unless of course you're fortunate to have a trailer with a ramp) but what you don't want to do is force the foal. They should be given time to think about it until they choose to join Mommy in there. If the foal views the trailer as something scary that they are being forced into, you're only creating problems down the road.

I actually didn't try loading Geo this way, mainly because the trailer we had at the time was a straight load with a non-removable center post, so it would have been difficult to get them both in this way. I think he was actually weaned before I tried loading him, but since he had been leading well from an early age, he followed me up into the trailer with only a brief pause to sniff the floor. Make sure the trailer is as bright as possible inside. Open any windows that you can so that it's not quite such a scary black box. Once you do get the foal inside, especially if you are loading them without their mother, hold them there for a few minutes and give them lots of praise before taking them back out. Don't try to do it all in one day, but work with them frequently, building up from just going in the trailer, to having the partition closed against them, to being tied up, etc. Perhaps feed them in the trailer to encourage positive association.

Geo's first actual journey in the trailer was when we went to his first show. In hindsight, I should have taken him for a ride first just to give him the experience of traveling, but he was so good about load-ing and standing in the trailer that I thought he would be fine about it, so I skipped this step. He loaded fine at home, and traveled okay (it

Kinda fuzzy-coated but still such a handsome boy.

was only about a half-hour trip) though didn't eat much of his haynet. For an eighteen-month-old colt who had never left home and was now surrounded by new sights, sounds, and horses, he behaved impeccably. Actually, his behavior was perfect for any young horse, colt or filly. I strongly recommend that until it's actually time for your class, you handle your young horse on a lunge line rather than just a lead line so that if they do become fractious you are much less likely to lose hold of them. Since he won his final class (okay, he was the only horse in that particular class, but I don't care, he still won!) he got to go into the championship class, where they pick Champion and Reserve for the division so far. The closest he came to acting up was when the steward literally ran at him with his blue ribbon for winning that one class, and he reared. Then, being the horse that he is, he dropped back down to all four feet and looked at me to see if he was in trouble. (He wasn't.) Who knows, maybe he was just excited to have won the class! But, as you can see from this next pic, he was *so* excited to be in the

Sure is tiring being this handsome!

championship class that he fell asleep with his chin in my hands during the lineup!

I guess the trailer ride had been a bit scarier than I realized, because Geo would *not* load up to come home. Maybe he was just enjoying the day out, but I don't think so. He just wouldn't get in the trailer. Unfortunately, it was just one of those situations where we needed one more person to make it work, and there were only two of us. Then, a lovely lady rode over on her horse and asked, very politely, if we could use another pair of hands. Of course, we said yes! (Hint: If someone offers help, never be too proud to take it! Also, if you see someone struggling, don't be afraid to offer help.) With this lady's assistance and advice, we got him loaded. Since Geo had been pulling back against the halter rope, she used my lunge line to make a body rope, looping it around his body behind the front legs with the end coming up between his front legs then through the halter so that if he pulled back he squeezed the rope on himself. This form of self-correction is very valuable when used correctly, since the horse simply has to stop pulling to release the pressure. With the body rope in place, she went into the trailer while I tried using a whip to get Geo to load. No, I was *not* beating him, but rather tapping rhythmically on his butt to try to irritate him into moving away from it. He did get a swat on the butt when he tried to move back or sideways, but otherwise we just let him think it through. We got him to the edge of the trailer and he was reluctant to step up so, since I know he's not a kicker, my husband and I linked hands behind his butt (Geo's butt, not my husband's) and just pushed him forward until he had to step up (he did try to fold himself in half first!). Once the front feet were in, he quit arguing about it and went all the way in where he was rewarded with copious amounts of carrots.

Very important whether your trailer is a straight load or a slant, you must always make sure that the rear door/ramp or partition is secured *before* you tie your horse up. This is especially important with a straight load trailer. The last thing you want to do is tie your horse up and then have them try to back out of the trailer! This is obviously extremely

Yes, I forgot to take off his tail bandage for the photo. I was still excited!

dangerous. Even if your trailer has a butt bar or chain behind them, they can still try to step back/down with this in place, so securely close the back of the trailer before you tie them up. Also, try to never be directly behind the door or ramp while you are closing it. I knew of someone who was killed when a horse they had just loaded kicked out while the ramp was being closed, slamming it back down onto the person's head.

Once we got Geo loaded and secured, we profusely thanked the kind lady for her help (in fact, I am still in contact with her) and got ourselves back in the truck to head home. So, the only bad part of Geo's first travel/show experience was my own fault, but at least it was bad insomuch as it was obviously a bit embarrassing that he wouldn't load when there were all those people around and nothing more.

Grooming

The foal can learn about being groomed from a very young age, but there's really no need to make a huge deal about it (Have you noticed yet that I try to not make *anything* a huge deal for the horse/foal?). Go into the stall, perhaps halter and tie mare and foal (if you've reached that stage with the foal), and groom the mare as you normally would. Then, use a soft brush (a body brush is fine) to gently brush the foal. You can think it more like dusting the foal at first. You aren't really trying to get them clean but just to get them used to the feel and the process. I definitely wouldn't use a mane/tail brush on their little mane and tail though, again just a light brushing with the body brush. This is also when you would normally pick feet, so make your farrier's life a bit easier and just pick up each foot, flick it with the brush of a hoof pick, maybe lightly scrape the pick over the sole or tap the sole so the foal becomes accustomed to the strange things humans do. Hopefully you have the time to groom your mare daily, or at least every other day, so work with the foal each time, gradually working up to a more normal grooming routine.

Bathing

The natural progression from grooming is bathing. This can be a little more challenging, but again I would use the mare as an example (assuming she is good for baths). Hose the mare down and let the foal get wet. I held Geo on his halter and rope and, while he was allowed to move around a bit, the one thing he has never been allowed to do is *leave*. By that I mean he stays in the general area where I want him until we're done. Some people recommend starting by gently hosing the lower legs and slowly working up to the body. Some advocate using a bucket of water and a sponge or rag to wet the foal down. My own experience with Geo was that he didn't like me hosing his legs too much, but he did like his body being hosed (maybe being in Florida helps—everyone appreciates a cold shower!). I also found that using a fairly heavy, "splashy" spray was better than a very fine spray. It seemed as though the fine mist felt more like insects than the one that was like, as Forrest Gump would put it, "big ol' fat rain." Of course, the hardest part to hose down is their heads, and I've always made it a practice to tell any of my horses, "face," and then spray their head. Geo was *not* a fan of this in the beginning, but I think the trick is not to stop when they back up or otherwise misbehave, because then all they are learning is that misbehavior means that whatever they dislike will stop. I keep spraying the head (with a gentle "rain" spray) and only when they stop moving will I praise and then stop the water. This helps to teach any horse that the easiest way to get it over with is to just let it happen.

When it comes to a proper bath, the easiest way to do this is to tie the foal (alongside the mare if they are still together) and treat it as bathing any horse. Hose them down, apply shampoo with whatever brush/mitt/sponge you prefer, then hose off the lather. Be gentle when using a sweat scraper to get the worst of the water off, and obviously don't use it on the legs or other bony parts. I found that Geo tended to stay pretty clean anyway, not sure if that's true of all foals, so for him bathing was more about learning to be bathed than getting off too much dirt.

Weaning

One of the most stressful times for your foal, and often for the mare, is weaning. You may think that nature will take care of that for you, and to some extent it does since the mare's milk quality and quantity will decrease somewhat over the months, but unless they are separated the foal *will* keep nursing for as long as they're able to reach under there. And if they are still nursing, the mare will still produce milk. In the wild, a foal will generally continue to nurse from the mare right up until just before she produces her next foal, so the foal will nurse for almost a year. The mare will only force weaning so that she is able to adequately provide for her new baby. This prolonged nursing can obviously take a lot out of the mare, so as humans, we intervene and enforce weaning at a younger age, generally at around six months. There are a couple different ways of doing this, and to some extent it will depend on your mare and foal since some are more dependent on each other and therefore require a greater separation.

The old-fashioned way of doing it was by removing the mares to a distant pasture and putting the foals into a large barn as a group to prevent them seeing the mares and trying to get to them. I know one Clydesdale breeder who would put the foal into an old-fashioned stone barn stall with no windows and keep both top and bottom doors closed until the foal stopped calling for the mare, which would take days or even a couple of weeks. That has always seemed a bit harsh to me (and this same breeder would at this point become very hands-on with the foal to try to transfer the foal's dependence from the mare to herself).

If you keep your mare and foal at home, this of course may limit your options. You could choose to move one of them temporarily to another property, thus keeping them far apart for a few weeks, but it is entirely possible that when they are reunited the foal may still try to nurse and, in so doing, stimulate the mare to lactate once more. You could put them in separate fields, but this could lead to one or both trying to get over/through the fence to reach the other.

So, what did we do?

Well, while we keep our horses at home, we are fortunate that we have a good solid barn and horses other than the mare and foal. Our preparations had started early. Back when Geo had to be kept from eating Moyie's grain, they had become accustomed to each being tied (loosely) by their buckets to eat their own meal. They had been spending their non-turnout time in the double-sized stall we had created, so on the day it was decided we would start weaning, while the whole herd was out together we rebuilt the dividing wall to make it into two stalls again. The way we had originally positioned the stall cameras meant that there was now one covering each of the stalls, which was just what we wanted. That evening, I put all the grain buckets into the stalls before I started bringing the horses in, and I simply led them into adjacent stalls where their buckets were waiting. Both of them are very food-oriented, so their immediate concern was in eating and not worrying too much about the wall between them. After they had eaten, there was some talking back and forth between them, but they were still able to see and touch each other through the upper rails of the wall, so there really wasn't much drama at all. Next day, they went out together again, and of course Geo immediately hit the milk bar, but by this stage it is really more of a comfort thing than actual nutrition. That night they were again separated, and I did this for a couple of days before finally putting Moyie out with the other mares while Geo stayed in his stall with his Thoroughbred buddy next door. Yes, there was some yelling and excitement, but since Moyie had a field to graze down and I gave Geo some nice yummy hay, their stomachs overruled anything else. Around lunchtime I brought the mares in and put the two boys out together with much the same result.

During the weaning period, you really don't have to change the foal's diet much, since by this stage they have been receiving most of their nutrition from grazing, hay, and grain, with the mare's milk simply a tasty supplement. The mare on the other hand needs to be "dried up," to stop her from producing milk. This is generally achieved by reducing her nutritional intake for a short time, usually by cutting out the grain portion of the ration and feeding only hay/grazing for a few days. When her milk production has ceased, or substantially reduced, you can begin feeding grain again, but now at a normal maintenance ration and not the much higher amount she was receiving as she fed the foal.

The udder will fill, and the mare may be uncomfortable as the foal is not suckling and reducing the size, but you must be watchful that she does not develop mastitis or a painful swelling of the udder. If she shows fever or her udder is hot to the touch or swollen (particularly just one side), you should contact the vet. You may also see a yellowish substance oozing from the affected teat. If mastitis is not treated quickly, the mare may become very ill and her udder may suffer permanent damage. This is clearly an issue if you plan to breed the mare again as her ability to produce milk will be severely impaired.

I made the mistake of reintegrating the herd after a week or two apart when Moyie still had milk, and Geo went right back to nursing. This simply confirmed that he could no longer be turned out with her at all, so our boy turnout/girl turnout became a permanent feature. In actual fact, Moyie continued to have milk in her udder for many months after Geo was weaned, and I think it was almost a year after weaning that she finally dried up! Her udder wasn't *full*, but there was definitely still milk present. My vet said not to worry about it as it sometimes happens. Some people will advocate that you milk the mare to reduce the amount of milk in the udder, which may be of comfort to the mare if her udder is very full, but milking her will stimulate lactation in the same way as the foal suckling would, so unless really necessary for the mare's comfort I wouldn't go this route.

It is important to note that before the foal is weaned, they are covered by the mare's Coggins certificate, but after weaning they will require their own Coggins test. The Coggins test is a simple blood test to check for Equine Infectious Anemia and must be carried out at least annually (some states require it more frequently). EIA is very infectious and any infected horses must be quarantined *for life*. It is illegal to transport a horse without a current negative Coggins certificate (unless it is an unweaned foal traveling with its dam) and it is also required that all horses on a commercial boarding facility possess a current negative Coggins. If you keep your horses at home and they never leave the property or have contact with other horses, you may not require a Coggins, but in the event that your horse needs to travel somewhere in an emergency, it's better to have it in hand. Besides, you're going to have your vet coming out to start your foal's vaccinations, so you may as well have them pull a blood sample while they're there.

Gelding

Gelding is only necessary if you have a colt foal which you do not intend to use as a stallion. We have kept Geo as a stallion, but if Geo had proven to have any kind of major conformational issues or poor temperament (which was very unlikely, given the temperaments of both his parents), he would have been gelded.[1] To be clear, if you do not intend to use him as a stallion, your colt should be gelded as early as possible. It is not cruel and, despite the old wives' tales to the contrary, gelding a colt early does not stunt their growth! Leaving the gelding process until he has reached a level of maturity where his hormones are already surging just makes your life more difficult. Horses mature at a very different rate from humans, and a two-year-old colt is often more than capable of successfully breeding a mare (and often even younger colts will be seen trying to mount their own mother).

I'll say it again. If you don't plan on him being a stallion, and aren't able or prepared to take on the responsibility of having a stallion, *geld your colt* as early as your vet recommends! As a sort of bonus point, research shows that the high levels of testosterone in a stallion cause the growth plates of the long bones to close earlier, meaning that if you geld your colt at a young age, he will likely mature into a taller horse than if he had been left entire.

It is preferable, from an infection-avoiding point of view, that the surgery not be done in the hottest part of the summer, and many people

---

1 The surgical procedure of gelding is also known as castration or cutting.

will have a colt gelded before he is weaned, so he has his mommy to comfort him in the recovery phase. It is a bit unfair to do it at weaning time, since the colt is already going through a stressful period, but some people will do it at this time. The process is fairly straightforward, basically the same as neutering a male dog, but there is generally no need for the colt to go to a veterinary hospital as the surgery can easily be done at your property. If the foal has not already been vaccinated, a tetanus vaccine is generally given at the time of the procedure, and some veterinarians may also choose to give anti-inflammatory and antibiotic drugs at this time as a prophylactic measure. A standard gelding operation like this is indeed a surgical procedure but usually without complications. After the procedure is complete, the anesthetic wears off and the horse will usually get to his feet in a half hour or so. They are often unsteady on their feet until fully conscious once more, so just be careful until he sobers up. Recovery "nursing" is fairly straightforward and focused on preventing infection and reducing swelling. For the first day after surgery, the gelding (sorry buddy, but you're no longer a colt!) should be kept in a stall or other confined area and monitored per your vet's instructions. This generally involves checking that the wounds aren't bleeding heavily (a little light dripping of blood is normal but streams of blood are not). If the horse seems colicky or otherwise ill, contact your vet.

After twenty-four hours you can start exercising your young gelding for short, controlled periods to help reduce swelling and stiffness. The wounds will heal from the inside out, but any major swelling of the scrotum which does not reduce with exercise may indicate infection. If your horse has a fever, is depressed, or won't eat, this could also indicate infection and your vet should be contacted. I know I seem to be skipping over the aftercare, but that's really because you should be taking guidance from your vet on this subject as they know your horse.

The surgery site will normally be fully healed in a few weeks, and over this period of time the hormone levels will change so that your horse's behavior may be markedly different by the time he is all healed up. Be aware that a recently gelded horse *may* still be able to impregnate a mare due to residual sperm in the urogenital tract, so he should be kept away from mares for thirty days post-surgery, though I think this is probably more of a concern if a colt is gelded later. If he is gelded prior to weaning, you may want to keep the mare and foal away from other mares during this time.

What I have covered is considered a "normal" gelding procedure. If a colt's testicles (one or both) have not descended normally, he may be referred to as a cryptorchid. The old names for this, still frequently used, were ridgeling or rig. These horses can still be gelded, and in fact probably *should* be gelded since cryptorchidism is a hereditary trait, but the procedure is a bit more involved. Castration of these horses is generally done at a veterinary hospital due to the more invasive and prolonged nature of the surgery.

Chapter 8

Weanling to Backing

AFTER the first six months or so of the foal's life, he or she is now a happy, healthy weanling. Once gelded, and after thirty days, the young gelding can be safely turned out with mares/fillies. If you have more than one foal, they can be turned out together now, but if you have a mix of colts and fillies, they really should be kept separate because it's still possible for even a very young colt to impregnate a young filly as soon as her heat cycles start. There have definitely been cases of pregnant yearling fillies because their pasture mate wasn't gelded! Being turned out with other horses is really important for the foal, which is something you should keep in mind if you are breeding at home and you only have the mare and foal. Not only for the foal's peace of mind, but also to keep them well mannered, since a horse will instill basic discipline far better than a human.

After weaning, the foal will have lost whatever nutrition it was still receiving from the mare's milk, so feed requirements will increase somewhat. With that said, the majority of the foal's ration should be given as forage, so either good grazing or ample hay (or both). A foal should receive no more than one pound of grain per day for each month of age, so at six months the foal's *maximum* grain intake should be six pounds per day. To be honest, I feel that's quite a lot, probably equaling one full scoop of grain twice a day (depending on your grain and the size of your scoop!) but if you are unsure, ask your vet's advice. You should monitor your foal's condition, and the easiest way to do this is to take regular photographs of the foal to ensure they are not becoming either fat or thin. Some foals will not eat well after weaning, while others will go the opposite way and get greedy, so just pay attention to what *your* foal is doing. If you are preparing your weanling for an immediate show career, you will want them a bit heavier than if they are being allowed a more natural growth, but always keep in mind that overweight is not healthy, and indeed by overfeeding at this time you may cause irreversible damage to joints, etc.

Due to the fact that feed amounts are calculated against bodyweight, and your growing weanling's bodyweight will be constantly changing, you should keep an eye on their overall condition and check their weight on a regular basis. Unfortunately, weight tapes don't tend to be as accurate for youngstock as they are for mature horses, and the commonly used Milner & Hewitt equation from 1969 isn't entirely accurate for younger horses, either. Some variations on the Milner & Hewitt equation may be more reliable for younger horses, as outlined below. In all cases, the horse is measured using a normal measuring tape (in inches) around the girth, over the wither, and just behind the front legs (this is known as the heart girth) and the length from point of shoulder to point of buttock.

Standard Milner & Hewitt equation:
(Heart girth^2 x body length) / 330 = weight in pounds

Variation for weanlings:
(Heart girth^2 x body length) / 280 = weight in pounds

Variation for yearlings:
(Heart girth^2 x body length) / 301 = weight in pounds

Bear in mind that what you are looking for is changes in bodyweight, so as long as you stick to the same calculation, you will pick up on any alterations. I would suggest doing this once a month, just to keep an eye on things. As the bodyweight increases, the feed ration should also be recalculated (though if your weanling is living at pasture with no additional grain being given, this isn't really an issue). Of course, bodyweight is important when it comes to dosage of things like dewormers, but even if these calculations aren't accurate to the pound, they will be close enough for this purpose as dewormer syringes are generally marked off in 250-pound increments. But, if you're unsure, consult your vet or even the manufacturer of the dewormer for their recommendation.

Vaccinations & Deworming

Always consult your vet when it comes to vaccinations, since requirements vary by country/region, but in the table below I'll lay out the recommendations I followed with Geo. Bear in mind that while this looks like a crazy long list, most of the time you (or your vet) will be giving combination vaccines which cover a bunch of different things in one shot. In other words, your poor baby is not going to feel like a pin cushion every time they see the vet! Note that these recommendations are for foals whose dams have been fully vaccinated prior to foaling. If your mare has not been vaccinated, or you are unsure of her vaccination status, the requirements may vary slightly and you should be guided by your vet's advice in this situation.

Disease	Vaccination Schedule[1]
Tetanus	3-dose series, given at: 4–6 months 4–6 weeks after first dose 10–12 months

---

1 Information taken from "Vaccinations for Foals" developed by the American Association of Equine Practitioners Infectious Disease Committee, 2008 and updated by the AAEP Biological & Therapeutic Agents Committee, 2012 and again updated by an AAEP Vaccination Guidelines Review Task Force in 2015.

Eastern/Western Equine Encephalomyelitis (EEE/WEE)	3-dose series, given at: 4–6 months 4–6 weeks after first dose 10–12 months
Rabies	2-dose series, given at: 6 months 4–6 weeks after first dose
West Nile Virus (WNV)	3-dose series, given at: 4–6 months 4–6 weeks after first dose* 10–12 months, prior to onset of next vector season *this may be required at 4 weeks after first dose, dependent upon vaccine type used*
Equine Herpesvirus (EHV)	3-dose series, given at: 4–6 months 4–6 weeks after first dose 10–12 months
Equine Influenza	3-dose series, given at: 6 months 3–4 weeks after first dose 10–12 months
Strangles (Streptococcus equi)	*Injected Vaccine* 3-dose series, given at: 4–6 months 4–6 weeks after first dose 4–6 weeks after second dose - OR - *Intranasal vaccine* 6–9 months 3–4 weeks after first dose 11–12 months

In the case of EEE/WEE and WNV, foals in the Southeastern USA should receive an additional vaccine dose due to early seasonal vector presence. EEE/WEE additional dose should be given at 2–3 months of age, while WNV is recommended at 2 months.

The list above is what I would consider core vaccinations but there are other diseases which your foal may be vaccinated against that are more of a risk-based requirement dependent upon your location and veterinary advice. Other possible vaccinations would be against: Anthrax, Botulism, Leptospirosis, Potomac Horse Fever (PHF).

Consult your vet for their deworming recommendations, because parasites also vary by country/region. I try not to overdo the deworming due to the problems of parasites becoming immune to chemicals. I also make sure that any new arrivals to our barn are dewormed on arrival. If you are introducing a new horse to your property and they will be turned out in the same pasture (even if not at the same time), they should be dewormed on arrival and kept in their stall for a day or two. This ensures that any parasites they poop out can be picked up in the stall cleaning and not distributed around the pasture. This protocol helps keep risk of parasites to a minimum, but it is still possible for the foal to pick up parasites from the mare or in even the best managed pasture, and since the damage from parasite infestation can be extensive, it's best to deworm to be on the safe side. The below is what I do/did, but consult your vet on this as everyone has different opinions and the most important thing is that your foal's long-term health and wellbeing are protected.

Age	Dewormer
2–3 months	Fenbendazole
4–6 months (before weaning)	Fenbendazole
It is recommended that a Fecal Egg Count (FEC) be carried out at weaning, to determine the type of parasite burden the foal is carrying, which will influence the choice of dewormer.	
9 months	Ivermectin & Praziquantel
12 months	Pyrantel pamoate

Good, appropriate feeding, appropriate vaccinations and deworming, regular farrier care (and by regular I mean every six weeks, not once a year!) are about all you need to do to your young horse. Equine dentistry is a bit more of a minefield of opinion these days, with some people (generally equine dentists) advocating for biannual checks and maintenance, and also for preemptive removal of wolf teeth, which are the vestigial first premolar teeth that lie directly in front of the long row of "chewing teeth" at the back of the jaw.

Registration

Assuming that your foal is eligible for registration with a breed society or similar organization, this is something you want to take care of as early as possible (in part because often the registration fees become a bit more expensive the older the horse is). Geo is registered with the American Paint Horse Association (APHA) so this is the one I'm most familiar with but all registries will differ somewhat, so you should check out the appropriate website for whichever organization you are going to register with to find out the exact requirements.

The stallion owner has to complete a breeding report for all the mares their horse bred each year, and this is submitted to the organization to record how many potential foals there will be. It is important to make sure before breeding that your chosen organization will accept the method of breeding used! No point breeding a lovely foal only to find out that because you used AI they are not eligible for registration.

If your mare is not registered with the organization, you need to take care of this, too. Quarter Horse and Thoroughbred mares can easily be added to the APHA list of mares for a small fee, and you can do this when submitting the foal registration, so long as you have the mare's papers showing you as the owner. The usual rule is that the owner of the mare at the time she has her foal is the foal's owner, so if you buy a pregnant mare, you, not the owner at time of breeding, are the foal's official owner.

After your foal is born, you need to fill out the paperwork with the details of both parents and the foal, plus the date/s of breeding. You will also have to submit clear photographs showing the foal from both sides, front and back so that all markings can be seen. (In the old days you would have had to draw the markings on a horse outline on the papers, and since Geo is a Paint I'm very glad that photos are now the way to go!) You also have to give a couple of options on the name you would like to register the foal as, in case there is already a horse registered with your first choice name (or the organization finds your choice unacceptable). Many times, people will try to include part of at least one of the parents' names, to give a tie back to the bloodline, but it's certainly not required. We registered Geo as "Moyie's Royal Outlaw." Moyie for his mom, Outlaw for his dad, and Royal for . . . well, I guess because he's our little prince! Anyway, the APHA accepted that one. Once the paperwork is completed, you can send it off with the photographs, any supporting papers (like copies of the mare's papers if necessary) and of course the registration fee. APHA returned our papers pretty quickly, which was great, but obviously certain times of the year are very popular for foaling/registration, so don't be surprised if it takes a few weeks.

Continuing Education

Something to always bear in mind with *any* horse is that in every interaction you have with the horse, you're teaching them something. Always make sure it's something you want them to learn! What do I mean by that? Well, take a really basic scenario. You are trying to work in your weanling's stall and they are constantly in your space. If you react by moving away from them or laughing it off as cute, you are teaching them that it's acceptable to push humans around and that they are essentially higher in the hierarchy than you are. Is this an opinion you want a grown horse to have? If, on the other hand, when they move into your space you move them back with a firm verbal reprimand and a firm push on the chest or shoulder if necessary, they will learn that this behavior is not acceptable. By being consistent in what you do or do not accept, they will quickly learn the rules. In fact, my own three-year-old stallion will move back when I take in his feed with only a look from me, because he was taught from day one that he moves where and when he is told.

Please don't mistake firm and corrective handling for being "mean" to the young horse. If you are worried about that, just observe how horses interact with one another, or how your mare disciplined her foal. Horses have a pretty strict herd hierarchy, and over the years I have found that they are much happier when they know who is in charge of things. Like the alpha mare of a wild herd who decides where they go and when, your horse/foal/weanling/yearling, etc. is comforted by an owner who sets boundaries and maintains them.

I believe with any horse it's helpful to practice a sort of "controlled stupidity." Yes, I know, another phrase that will have you going "Huh?" What I mean is that I try to not be overly careful around any horse. As an example, a lot of people will be ultra-careful about, say, blankets. They will be very gentle and slow about putting them on and taking them off "so they don't spook the horse." I certainly don't twirl the blanket around like a matador, but I will throw the blanket on a bit roughly, and I'll let the straps, etc. trail across their body when taking the blanket off without folding it carefully first. Why? Controlled stupidity, I think, makes a horse a bit more willing to pause and think. Maybe it's my own version of the ever-popular (and somewhat contentious) desensitizing! I just know that I can do silly things like throwing a tarp over a two-year-old colt's head and his biggest concern will be whether he can still get to the grass. Did he like it? Probably not a whole lot, but it also didn't seem to bother him that much. Did he accept it as not a run-for-your-life situation? Yes, because I said it was fine and I was right there with him. I will still routinely put empty shavings bags on his head and the only reaction I get is a long-suffering and rather bored look.

Whether it be training or controlled stupidity, the biggest thing to be aware of is how your horse is reacting. Nervous is fine, and confused is fine, but scared is not. The point of doing these things is not to frighten the horse, but to provide constant reassurance that, no matter what, you've got their back. A horse which feels safe and trusts its handler/owner will be far more willing to try "scary" things if that person is telling them it's safe to do so. This is also why I make a habit of (gently) bumping a horse with the butt end of my muck fork when cleaning around them, so that if it happens accidentally, they don't react badly. They need to understand that things will bump them or touch them or land on top of them, and that it's okay.

There are lots of things that you can and will without realizing it teach your youngster, which is why you must always keep in mind that their training is a continuous process. I try to allow any horse a degree of leeway in their behavior so that I can gauge whether they have really learned what I have taught them. For instance, I will routinely lead my adult horses between the barn and field with just a rope around their necks, because they are respectful enough that nothing more is generally required. I try to work with the lightest amount of restraint possible so that if a horse becomes difficult or pushy, I can increase the control very easily. I will also occasionally revert to *all* of my horses being led and turned out "properly," using halter and rope, taking them into the field and turning them to the fence before removing the halter. Just as a sort of reminder of what is expected. I handle Geo in a halter and rope simply because he is still much earlier in his training and is also a three-year-old stallion walking past a bunch of mares and I don't think it's fair on him to push his manners too far. I always handle the adult stallion we have here in the same manner, and will always handle a stallion in a halter just as a matter of good practice.

There are so many things for a young horse to learn that I'm not going to exhaustively go through every one, but the important things to remember are to teach *and keep on teaching* your horse to lead politely, to tie up quietly and safely, and to accept grooming, hoof care, farrier care, and bathing without too much adverse behavior. Farrier care can be especially difficult for young horses, because even if you are cleaning their feet every day, you're not holding the leg up for as long or in such a tight way as the farrier must. Bearing in mind that horses are prey animals whose weapon of choice when threatened is to run away, it is asking a lot of trust for your young horse to stand while a relative stranger holds them helpless with a leg in the air. So, yes, they should accept the process, but I also think you need to cut them a little slack in the beginning as they become accustomed to the sensation of their hoof being cut and rasped. It isn't so much that they *feel* the hoof being cut, but the vibration of the rasp can unsettle them.

A lot of young horses (and older ones) don't like getting their shots done, and if you look at the size of the needles used, I really can't blame them! You can only try to get it done as safely and painlessly as possible, and if that means you must apply a twitch to make them stand so it can be done, then so be it. I have found that using a shoulder/neck twitch is very effective on some horses, and much easier to do than using a traditional nose twitch (which I have found sometimes encourages rearing anyway). I can shoulder twitch Geo with my left hand and give the shot with my right which seems to work for us. It's a bit hard to explain how to do the shoulder twitch, so please ask your vet to show you how to do it! Like everything else, whether you do the shots yourself or are just holding the horse for your vet, it should be treated as a "this is happening" situation and not made into a bigger deal than it needs to be. The more you act like it's scary, the more your horse will respond in the same way.

The more your young horse is handled, the better. If you have the time, and I'm very aware that we don't always have the time to do all the things we "should" or want to with our horses, try to halter, tie, and groom them each day. The more it's done, the more it will become just part of their normal life. The one thing to not neglect, though, is insisting on correct behavior. If you lead your weanling out to the field in the morning before you leave for work, don't view it as "just putting them out in the field" and accept poor behavior because you're in a hurry to leave. A horse will quickly learn that they can rush to the field or barge through the gate, which can quickly escalate to trying to break free of you. If it means you have to get up a few minutes earlier to make sure you can properly halter, safely lead, and turn loose, then do it! Basic manners should never be neglected as this can too easily lead to bigger problems.

Where you are located will to a large extent determine whether or not you use blankets on your horses, but if you do, the young horse should be introduced to this process with a little care (before you work up to the controlled stupidity mentioned before). I prefer to not tie the horse up when putting on blankets. If the blanket is the closed-front style, I will first fold it in half then in half again to make it a bit narrower, then stand by the shoulder and hold the blanket open to lift it up and over the horse's face, moving it quickly enough that the horse isn't "blinded" for too long, but also not whipping it up and over in a frightening way. Once over the ears, slide it down the neck to the shoulder. As the horse gets more used to it, I will sometimes hold the blanket over their face a little longer, just to accustom them to having their eyes covered. I will also often just fold the blanket once so that it takes longer to pass over the head. Yet again, the key is to be safe and act in a no-nonsense way.

Your main focus for the first two to three years of your young horse's life is simply keeping them healthy with appropriate vaccinations and hoof care, etc. alongside providing clear and consistent handling to encourage and maintain good manners. There are so many new experiences and things for a young horse to learn that the more they can be exposed to at an early age, the better.

Backing/Starting under Saddle

Now we're getting into the realm of starting a young horse on a working career, and this can be a pretty controversial subject so, as with everything else in this book, you'll get my personal opinion. I believe that a youngster can and should get used to things being put on them and around their bellies, in preparation for saddling (or harnessing, if your baby is to be a driving horse). This starts with blankets, though, since some of them (especially foal blankets) have a single belly strap. If your foal has been accustomed to wearing a blanket now and then, the pressure of a strap around their girth area shouldn't be too scary. I put a saddle on Geo when he was only about nine months old. I used a very lightweight, small saddle, girthed it only tight enough for safety (so it didn't move when he did) and led him around. He was utterly unimpressed by the whole experience. I do *not* believe in starting to

ride a horse until they are at
least three years old, and even
then, only very lightly. Geo
is now almost four, and we
are only now starting more
serious work. He has been
long reined (sometimes called

ground driving or long lining) a few times and we are starting to try
out lunging. I much prefer long reining to lunging with a young horse,
because constantly going in circles is tough on their joints, and I feel
like long reining gets them more accustomed to the feel of the bit and
of things bumping along their sides. He has worn a saddle a few times,
and I have also messed around with him, lying/sitting on his back when
he's napping and a couple of times climbing up on a stool and lying
across his back while he's standing in his stall. Nothing very much at
all. Many people will start a horse under saddle at two, but I just don't
agree with it. You need to give a young horse's bones and joints time
to mature before adding the strain of a rider and work. Many, *many*
people start horses young, and that's their choice, but it's not for me. If

all goes to plan, I would like to take Geo to a dressage show or two next year, just to do a couple of walk/trot classes. As much as I know he has scope for jumping, I do not intend to jump him under saddle until he is probably five years old.

All of the following training suggestions (well, other than just getting the horse accustomed to being saddled/bridled) are usually done in a fenced arena, round pen, or other confined area so that if your horse does get out of control at any stage, they aren't going to go very far or get into too much trouble if they get away from you. If you don't have a suitably enclosed area, you can still start your horse, but you just need to be a little more careful. Try to work in the safest area you have available to you.

I prefer long reining to lunging, but before you get to that, the young horse first needs to get used to the feel of a bit in their mouth. As with the saddle, I put a bit in Geo's mouth fairly young, just to see what he thought of it. And, as with the saddle, the answer was not too much. In general, I prefer double-jointed bits (my favorite is an Albacon loose ring French link snaffle), as they don't pinch the tongue and also give a clearer aid on each side of the mouth to make steering easier. The only downside of double-jointed bits, really, is that it can be easier for a horse to get their tongue over the bit to evade the pressure. I find that putting the bit maybe one hole higher than would be usual can help with this until a horse gets used to the feel of metal in their mouth. This doesn't make the bit excessively high or uncomfortable, but it serves the purpose. You don't need a youngster to get into bad habits right at the start.

The first time I put the bit in Geo's mouth, I didn't use a bridle but just hooked my fingers into the bit rings and lifted it up in the same way I would normally put on a bridle. Once he took the bit into his mouth, I raised it into the correct position and just held it there for a few moments, then let him drop it again. This way, if he took a strong dislike to it being there, it wasn't stuck on a bridle and hard to remove. Also, the motion of putting the bridle over the ears will move the bit a little higher for a moment, and I just wanted to see his reaction to the metal in his mouth. As per Geo-normal, he was completely underwhelmed.

The next step was to actually put a bridle on him. First, I laid the bridle onto his head without a bit to check that the cheekpieces were about the right length. You don't want to adjust them a whole lot once it's on their head and the bit is in their mouth. Having satisfied myself that it was close enough, I attached the bit to the bridle and put it on in the way I always do: Right arm around the bridge of the nose, hand holding the bridle against the front of the face; left hand holding the bit open and offering it up to the mouth. If necessary, your left thumb can push in at the corner of the mouth to encourage opening, then raise your right hand to bring the bit into the mouth and get the headpiece over the ears, then stop. Don't worry about fastening the throatlatch or anything else. Just let the horse think about it. Obviously, if it becomes apparent that the bit is too low or too high, you can try to adjust it without removing the bridle. I give them a few minutes to play with and mouth the bit, and I generally find that if it's in the correct position, they stop messing around with it pretty quickly. If everything seems good, fasten the throatlatch (and noseband if there's one on the bridle) and just let them stand and think. Don't leave them alone with the bridle on, but maybe go ahead and brush them or perhaps clean the stall. You just want to stay close in case they start trying to rub the bridle on walls or on their legs. Leave it on for five or ten minutes, then unfasten the throatlatch and noseband.

Removing the bridle correctly and safely is just as important as putting it on properly, as this is often something which can become an issue. I like to put my right hand on the horse's poll, under the bridle, then use my left hand to lift the headpiece up and forward over the ears while my right hand keeps the head steady as I lower the bridle gently and let them open their mouth to drop the bit. Try not to let the bit bang against their teeth and definitely try to prevent them from throwing their head up (hence the hand on top of the head) as this can be dangerous. I had a horse do that to me once, pulling free with the bit still in her mouth and running off with the bridle dangling around her front legs. She dropped the bridle after a short distance, but the damage was done: one broken bridle and one horse who took many months of patient work to get her back to letting me remove her bridle in a normal way.

Saddling for the first time should, in my mind, be done with the same lack of fuss as bridling. I've already briefly mentioned that Geo wore a saddle for a short time at a pretty young age, but with no intent to ride him, only to see his reaction. I prefer not to tie a horse for this, but just put on their halter and lead rope. If you have a helper, have them hold the horse loosely, or if you're working alone like me, just drape the rope over your forearm/elbow while you work. I don't mind if the horse moves a little bit as I'm saddling for the first few times, because what I don't want is that they feel trapped, as this can cause far more stress than is needed. As you'll have noticed with most things I've written about Geo, he was vastly unimpressed with the whole experience. I saddled him in the barn aisle, then took him for a walk around and out into the field, let him graze for a few minutes, then took him back to the barn. If you do this, be as smooth, slow, and gentle as you can, but snug that girth up securely because nothing will ruin a first saddling experience more than the saddle ending up on the horse's side or belly!

To remove the saddle, you can follow the textbook procedure of unbuckling the girth on the left side and gently dropping it, then going to the right side and unbuckling the girth there, taking it off completely and laying it over the saddle, then securing it under the stirrup irons before going to the left side again and carefully lifting the saddle up and off. Or you can do what I do with any horse. Unbuckle the girth on the left side, let it fall, if it bangs on their legs, no biggie, grab the front and back of the saddle (and saddle pad if you have one on there), lift a little, and pull it toward you. Let the girth slither over their back until you can grab it. Again, controlled stupidity. The bigger deal you make of something, the more reactive your horse will be.

The simplest thing to do when introducing a young horse to wearing a bridle it to use just a bridle, with no reins attached. But if, like me, you're doing it on a whim one day and the bridle you're using has reins, then you certainly don't want to leave them loose on a baby (or any other horse for that matter). If the bridle does have reins attached then, as with any horse, you should have put the reins over their neck before you put the bridle on. Before you buckle the throatlatch, take hold of one rein in each hand, under the horse's neck. Pushing them away from you, pass the left rein over the right, then push the right rein over the left and repeat until the reins are twisted together. Now take the long end of the throatlatch and pass it through the space between the reins where your hands are. It must go between the reins, not just under them! Buckle up your throatlatch and the reins will be held securely up against the neck. When you want to use the reins, just unbuckle the throatlatch and let the reins fall loose (then buckle the throatlatch again). This is also how I tie up reins if I am lunging a horse with reins on the bridle.

When it comes to tacking up, do it when you can, do it when you have time. You don't want to rush through it. A simple but very wise thing I once heard about working with horses: Act like you've got all day, and it'll take five minutes. Act like you've got five minutes and it will take all day! Like anything else, don't be in a rush. Do things correctly and in a routine and speed will come.

If you feel you're getting out of your depth, get a good trainer involved. First impressions are important, and even more so when it comes to a young horse's first impressions of work. Do not be so proud that you refuse to seek help until you have actually caused a major problem. To be honest, if you are worried about the process, if you've never started a young horse before, give serious consideration to having them started by a professional. Find one who will involve you in the process, so that you can learn what they do (or not, if you just want the horse started under saddle and are happy to pass that piece of the puzzle along to someone else). I have always said that, if I encounter difficulties with Geo, I will happily get someone else to help me.

If you do think of sending your baby away for starting and backing, make certain that you are happy with the trainer's reputation not only for horse starting but also horse care. If a trainer tells you that you are not allowed to visit your horse while it is being started, I would strongly advise against using that trainer. I wouldn't want to be some kind of helicopter horse-parent, but I would want to be sure that my horse was being treated in a way I found acceptable if popped in unexpectedly.

I long reined Geo a bit in just a halter, but you have very little real control, and the last thing you want them to learn is that they can just run from you. I'm not much of a runner anyway, but I *know* I couldn't keep up with a cantering Geo, so it's much preferable to have a mild bit in their mouth to do this. I suggest using a training surcingle for this, as these have multiple rings for attaching things or, in this case, running the reins through. I like to use the rings just either side of the wither for long reining, as it keeps the reins nice and high and also quite close to the rider's hand height. Using the reins on the lower rings doesn't give the same feel (and some horses will quickly learn to tuck their chin in and use their shoulders to avoid listening to you if the reins are on the lower rings). Wear a helmet and gloves when long

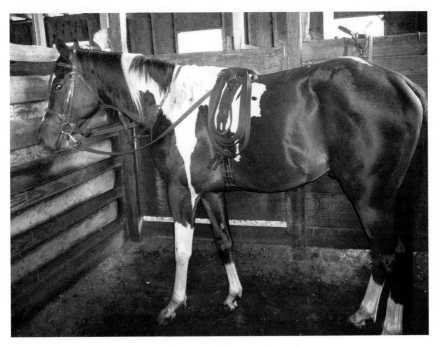

reining. To start with, having a helper is, well, helpful. You, as the long reiner, want to stand behind and slightly to one side of the horse. You should be close enough that you have good control, but far enough back that a kick won't reach you! The helper can have a lead rope attached to the horse to help at the beginning, since this is how your baby has been accustomed to being led.

From the beginning, I made a point to use two words to Geo for directions. If I wanted him to turn left, like turning to me when I was putting him in the field, I would say "come." To turn right, I would say "away." The words don't matter. You can use "sausages" and "French fries" if you like. The important thing is consistency. Using the same words for the same thing from day one means that they are ingrained in your horse's head and can therefore be used to help them understand when you are long reining (or riding).

Your helper should stay as passive as possible, just there if backup is needed. You can use a driving type whip if you like, but while I do carry one during long reining, it's generally tucked behind me. Praise when they get it right. Lots of "good boy/girl" when they do what they're asked. Correct them when they're wrong (that's where the "no" comes in). Walk a little, ask for a halt. Remember two things about long reining a youngster. One, using long reins gives you a whole lot of leverage on the bit, so be very gentle. Two, their mouths are very sensitive, especially when they are just being started, so be very, *very* gentle. You want to encourage them to obey, never force. If they don't stop when asked, your helper should assist (and in many cases a horse who has been taught to lead well will stop if the helper just stops walking). Also, don't expect a "trained horse" reaction speed. Give the command clearly and give them a chance to process and react before you decide to try again.

Once the young horse gets the hang of starting and stopping, introduce steering into the equation. Again, the length of your reins will cause great leverage on the bit, so I try to just vibrate my fingers on the side where I want them to turn, while using whichever word you have taught them for that direction. In Geo's case, a left turn means vibrating the fingers of my left hand while repeating "come." Don't *pull* the horse around, but give them time to understand what the pressure on the bit on one side means. As your horse's understanding grows, your helper can take off the lead rope and move further away until they are no longer needed.

As with teaching anything, whether to a horse, a human, or a dog, the key thing is consistency and repetition. But don't overwork a young horse, even just on long reins. Work long enough to get some good responses to your commands, then stop. The purpose of this is not to exhaust the horse, or to improve fitness, but to teach commands. Once the commands have been learned and responses given correctly, don't keep plugging away because if your horse thinks they have done what was asked of them yet you keep on asking, they may start to doubt their responses were correct and give incorrect ones in an attempt to satisfy you. Get the desired results, then stop for the day. Do it again the next day, or the day after that.

You can of course also trot a horse on long reins, but only if you're prepared to jog along behind them. You can also move from long reining to lunging with two reins, but this is something best learned from watching it done correctly, not trying to figure it out from a book. If you do choose to lunge your youngster, whether on a lunge line (which I prefer) or loose in a round pen, do *not* overdo it! Their joints cannot withstand extended periods of running around in tight circles without sustaining damage.

Once the long reining controls are established and your horse is responsive, you can progress to long reining with the saddle on. Some people will let the stirrups down and run the reins through the irons, but this is putting the reins very low on the horse. I suggest, if possible, putting the training surcingle over the saddle so you can still use the rings as before. If it won't fit, try attaching carabiner clips or something similar to the D rings on the front of almost every saddle and running the reins through those. This should of course only be done if you are sure that your horse will not fight against the reins, because while the D rings are intended for attaching things like breastplates, they are

probably not going to withstand a fighting horse. When appropriate, guided by
your horse's behavior, I would then long
rein with the stirrups loose. The more
frequently you work with the horse, the
quicker they will progress, but so long as
their education is moving forward in the
correct way, progress is progress.

In preparation for backing, you
should get the horse used to you being
above them, and for this a good solid
mounting block is very helpful. The
heavy plastic movable ones are really good for this, because instead of
fussing around trying to get the horse perfectly positioned next to a
fixed block, you can get them standing squarely then bring the block to
them, at least initially. If you have a helper who can assist, great. If you
are working alone, it's always a good idea to let someone know what
you're doing. Get the horse positioned with the block at their left side,
as though you were going to mount. Climb up on the block and just
scratch/pat/rub the horse's neck and back, reaching as far toward their

tail as you can. Patting and rubbing, especially around the croup and hindquarters, will get them accustomed to being bumped in this area, so that if a rider inadvertently kicks them in the butt while mounting or dismounting, it won't be such a big deal to the horse.

Let me pause for a moment. Please, *please* wear a helmet when training your young horse. I know, they can be hot and annoying, but *any* horse can put a foot wrong, even inadvertently. Try Googling Courtney King-Dye. This young woman was an Olympic dressage rider, until a horse she was riding at home (without a helmet) stumbled and fell. Courtney suffered a traumatic brain injury which almost killed her, but instead left her with permanent physical damage. It doesn't matter how experienced you are, accidents can happen and wearing a helmet isn't *that* onerous.

You want to work on letting more and more of your weight rest on the horse's back until you reach a point where you can lift your feet off the block and let your entire weight lie on the horse's back. I like to do this at first without a saddle, partly because I think it's probably less

uncomfortable for the horse and partly because I *know* it's less uncomfortable for me to lie across a bare back than a saddle. Next step would be adding the saddle. I think it's best to tack up and long rein the horse in the saddle before repeating what was done bareback. Taking the stirrups off the saddle will make things more comfortable for you. Stand up on a mounting block and pat/rub all over before laying your weight gradually onto the saddle and work up to laying your full weight on it. The next bit will require a helper, who should also be *wearing a helmet*! You then want to repeat the lying-across-the-saddle exercise, but this time make sure your weight is fairly evenly balanced so you don't slide. Then, your helper should gently ask the horse to walk forward with you lying on the saddle. Don't be surprised if the horse is hesitant, because this is the first time that they have felt the extra weight moving around as they walk. Have them walked a short distance then stop and give lots of praise. If all is going well, another short walk. By doing this lying across the saddle, if the horse does throw a tantrum, you are in a position where you can easily, and relatively safely, slide to the ground. After a couple of short walks like this, end the session by sliding to the ground. Make sure to keep talking to your horse, and make sure your helper remains alert while you are getting off the horse, as the sudden weight shift can be a bit unsettling to them.

Congratulations! You have now reached the point where, in the old days, you could say your horse had been "backed." Of course, there is still a lot to be done, but I believe that walking calmly with the dead weight of a human lying on their backs is a huge step in any horse's education, so give yourself a pat on the back while you're patting your horse. (And please always remember that this "do this, then this, then move on to this" is condensing the whole thing into assuming that everything goes right every time! If something takes a few sessions to get right, so be it. Take the time now and it will pay off in the long run. Don't try to rush through the basics just to get to the "fun" part of riding. If you do, an unprepared, un-ready horse is likely to give you much more "fun" in your first rides than you really want!)

In your next session, you should repeat the lying on the saddle and being led at walk. After that, well, you know what comes next: Getting on and sitting astride your homebred youngster. For this you will obviously want the stirrups to be attached to the saddle, so I would suggest that they are allowed to dangle at the horse's sides during the initial warm-up long reining and lying across. By this time your horse should be well accustomed to feeling them banging against their sides anyway. Make sure the girth is tight enough, too.

Use the mounting block (I will always try to use a mounting block or something else to get on any horse as it's easier on their backs) and put your foot in the left stirrup as you normally would. Press your weight on the stirrup so the horse can feel the saddle tilt sideways a bit. Do this a few times, then your helper (your helmet-wearing helper!) should move to the right side of the horse. While they maintain control of the horse via the lead or lunge line, they should take hold of the right stirrup leather to hold the saddle steady. Some people will put their hand into the iron, but I find this awkward (and a little dangerous as they could potentially get caught up). I prefer to wrap my left hand under the leather about halfway down the saddle flap which allows me to put pressure on the stirrup but then easily and smoothly slide my hand down as the rider mounts so I can turn the iron for them to put their foot in.

In this first-mounting situation, though, I do not try to get my foot into the right iron immediately. I want to stand on my left stirrup with one hand on the horse's wither and the other on the seat of the saddle (*not* the cantle), then pause and give a pat and a few reassuring words (to the horse, not the helper). Then, swing your right leg up and over the hindquarters before lowering yourself gently into the saddle. Do not thump down like a sack of potatoes but lower your weight as lightly as possible. Let your right leg hang down the horse's side and take another pause to pat and reassure. If your horse fidgets a little, don't reprimand them, since they are trying to adjust their balance to cope with your weight. When they stand quietly, your helper can assist you in putting your right foot into the stirrup (the normal way of "fishing" for it can be upsetting to the young horse at first). Your helper can now move to the left side of the horse, and they may want to move the mounting block out of the way at this point, or find another helper who can do it for you. (Let's face it, the chances are pretty good that you will have someone taking photos as you have your first sit on your young horse, so they can pause for a minute and move the block.)

Take hold of the reins very loosely. At this stage your helper has control and you are just, for want of a better description, a crash test dummy. I recommend either having a lead rope secured around the horse's neck that you can hold along with the reins, or using a short strap fastened to the front D rings of the saddle. Depending on who I am talking to, I either call this a chicken strap (if talking to kids) or an "oh shit" strap (if talking to adults, because that's probably what you'll be saying if you suddenly have to grab it!). Regardless of what you call it, holding this while keeping a gentle hold of loose reins will mean that if there are any stumbles, etc., you will be pulling on a strap or rope, *not* your horse's mouth.

Sit as straight and upright as possible, basically sit in the best position you have, and allow your helper to walk the horse forward. The horse may be hesitant again, as your weight is now very differently distributed than when you were lying on the saddle, but if you have covered the basics well then there should (hopefully) be no major tantrums. As before, walk a little, then stop, walk a little, then stop. If all is going well, you can take your hands off the strap and hold your reins more normally, perhaps shortening them a little bit, too.

Maybe for the next halt, you could give the command yourself. I find this most effectively done in a classical dressage type way. Excuse my description, kids and adults both find it funny, but it conveys what is needed without confusing the instruction. First thing you want to do is deepen your seat, pressing evenly down into the saddle while stiffening your back so you no longer follow the horse's movement. I know, you're trying to figure that out, right? Well, how about this instead. Imagine you're pooping on the saddle. (Cue giggles.) I'm serious. If you just imagine you are pooping on the saddle, you will push your seat down and stiffen your back. If you don't believe me, try it just sitting on a chair. Your seat bones push down and your core tightens, stiffening your back. So, stop giggling and use that image. The other thing I like to describe, rather than pulling on the reins, is to try to touch your shoulder blades together. It gives a bit of resistance on the bit without an actual "pull." To be honest, in a young horse with an unspoiled mouth, that should be all that is needed. And say "whoa" (or whatever word you have chosen to make your "whoa" command).

If the halt goes to plan, lots more praise to your baby horse, then try the accelerator. Lightly touch the horse's sides with your lower legs as you say "walk." If they don't respond, repeat the aid while your helper walks forward. Always remember that the young horse has a lot to learn, and you must be patient with them. There's no point getting annoyed or aggressive when they simply don't know what legs-bumping-my-sides means. That's why you use the vocal command which they already know along with the leg aid, so they will associate the two commands. Again, when you do get the desired result, lots of praise.

If walking and halting are working, you can try out the steering, which should hopefully be fairly well established if you have been long reining your youngster. Again, be gentle. When I teach people to ride, I encourage them to turn like one of those little Lego-man figures. Remember those? More specifically, remember how they joined together at the waist? So, turn like one of those. Your lower body remains still, but turn from your waist to look where you're trying to go. Yes, the correct sequence of commands is to put a little more weight on the inside seat bone, a little pressure on the inside leg while the outside leg slides back a fraction, the inside hand comes back a little as the outside hand allows the turn . . . that's a lot to remember. But if you allow your entire upper body to turn like a Lego man, you're actually doing *all* of that, but only having to think of one thing.

The key, in my mind, is to keep all aids as light as possible to achieve the desired result. You know when you watch a great rider and think the horse is superbly trained because the rider "isn't doing anything," then you ride that same horse and can't make it walk a straight line? That's because the first rider *is* giving commands, but they're giving them clearly and very subtly so it appears they are doing nothing. One of the things I hear when I'm riding which makes me super happy is when someone says, "How did you make him/her do that? You didn't do anything." Yay! Subtle commands with appropriate response achieved!

Now, if your first session riding astride can produce quiet and obedient responses to halt, walk, and turn in both directions, I would stop there and dismount. Next session you can forgo the lying over the saddle and just mount carefully. Maybe next session your helper can remove the rope and just walk alongside, gradually moving further away.

Keep your early riding sessions short, and I would suggest walking for a few rides before introducing trot. It is easier on a young horse's back (well, any horse's back) if you rise to the trot, though some do seem to find it a little unbalancing, so in this case perhaps even take a forward seat/two-point position where your seat is out of the saddle and hovering over it. This can be a somewhat less effective position, especially if you aren't stable in this position, and even more especially if you are unstable and the horse stumbles (or bucks!). Take it slow and steady when training your young horse and try not to push too far too fast. Listen to your horse and never ride them to the point of being over tired. The quality of the time spent riding is far more important than the quantity of time spent.

"FOAL WATCH" COOKIES

I promised you a cookie recipe, didn't I?

Ingredients

4 oz butter

4 oz brown sugar

3 oz white sugar

1 egg

1 tsp vanilla extract

9 oz all-purpose flour

1 tsp baking soda

Chocolate chips/caramel chips/nuts/whatever else you fancy!

Instructions

1. Preheat oven to 350°F.
2. Cream butter and sugars.
3. Add egg and beat in thoroughly.
4. Add vanilla and mix well.
5. In a separate bowl, sift together flour and baking soda and add mix gradually to wet ingredients.
6. Stir in chips/nuts/whatever you're using (I love white chocolate and chopped macadamias).
7. Drop rounded teaspoonfuls of mixture onto a lightly greased cookie sheet and bake 8–10 minutes. (Test by pressing lightly on a cookie. It should dent just a bit as they will sink and harden a little as they cool.)
8. Cool on wire rack (however many you don't eat straight from the oven) and enjoy while waiting for a mare to foal!

Epilogue

OKAY, so one other thing I'll tell you about. I already said that I didn't start Geo's education as a riding horse until he was over three years old, but there was one grown-up thing he did get to do. As well as Moyie (and Geo) we also have a beautiful eighteen-year-old Quarter Horse mare named Barbie (Color WithinTheLines), and we wanted to try getting a foal from her. As she is a bit on the older side for a first time mommy, though, we didn't want to put a lot of pressure on trying to get her pregnant, so we decided that instead of sending her off to a stallion or anything else like that, we would simply put her and Geo in the same field for a few months (starting in the winter) and see if nature took its course when spring came around and she started coming into heat again.

It took a while, and quite a lot of Barbie making it clear that she was *not* in the mood, but eventually she came into heat and became receptive to Geo's advances (you may have already caught this turn of events in some of the photos used in the book). So, long story short, it would appear that their very first mating caused pregnancy (not bad for a young stallion) as when my vet performed an ultrasound on Barbie fifteen days after the first breeding, she was definitely pregnant (yes, that was her ultrasound you saw).

So now we're back into the waiting game, but this time waiting for an even more homebred foal, since this one will be out of one of our mares *and* by our homebred stallion. Guess that means Moyie will be a grandma! Foal is due May 5th, 2020, just after this book releases, so keep your fingers crossed for us!

Index